Happy-Go-Lucky

Also by David Sedaris

Happy-Go-Lucky

David Sedaris

Little, Brown and Company

New York Boston London

Little, Brown and Company
Hachette Book Group
1290 Avenue of the Americas, New York, NY 10104
littlebrown.com

First Edition: May 2022

Little, Brown and Company is a division of Hachette Book Group, Inc. The Little, Brown name and logo are trademarks of Hachette Book Group, Inc.

The publisher is not responsible for websites (or their content) that are not owned by the publisher.

Acknowledgment is made to the following, in which the stories in this collection first appeared, some differently titled or in slightly different form: *The New Yorker:* "Active Shooter," "Father Time," "Hurricane Season," "Unbuttoned," "The Vacuum," "Pearls," "Happy-Go-Lucky," "A Better Place," "Lucky-Go-Happy"; *The Paris Review:* "A Speech to the Graduates"; *Elle:* "Highfalutin"; Amazon Original Stories: "Themes and Variations"; *Vogue UK:* "Smile, Beautiful."

ISBN 9780316392457 (hc) / 9780316445412 (large print)
LCCN 2021945760

Printing 1, 2022

LSC-H

Printed in the United States of America

For Ted Woestendiek

Ban everything. Purify everything. Moral cleanse everything. Anything that was bad or is bad, destroy it. Especially in the forest, where you live your life as a tree, wielding an axe.

—Sigmond C. Monster

Contents

Contents

Happy-Go-Lucky

Active Shooter

It was spring, and my sister Lisa and I were in her toy-sized car, riding from the airport in Greensboro, North Carolina, to her house in Winston-Salem. I'd gotten up early to catch my flight from Raleigh, but still she had me beat by an hour. "I like to be at Starbucks right when they open, at five a.m.," she said. "Speaking of which, I was there a few months ago and saw a lady with a monkey. I don't know what kind, but it was small—not much bigger than a doll—and was in a pink frilly dress. And it was just so...upsetting to me. I wanted to go up to this woman and ask, 'What do you plan on doing with that thing once you lose interest in it?'"

Like a lot of pet owners I know, Lisa is certain that no one can take care of an animal as well as she can. "Look at how that guy is dragging his Irish setter on that leash!" she'll say, pointing at what to me just looks like a man walking his dog.

Or, if the dog is *not* on a leash: "That beagle's about to be hit by a car, and his owner's not doing a thing about it." No one's spaniel has the shots it needs. Nobody's bird is eating correctly or getting its toenails trimmed to the proper length.

"What made you so sure this woman was going to lose interest in her monkey?"

Lisa gave me the look that said, *A monkey—of course she's going to lose interest in it,* and said, "A monkey—of course she's going to lose interest in it."

It was right around there that we came upon a billboard for a firing range called ProShots.

"I think we should go to that place and shoot guns," Lisa said.

And so it was that on the following afternoon we arrived for our three o'clock appointment. I had assumed for some reason that a firing range would be outdoors, but instead it was situated in a strip mall, next to a tractor-supply store. Inside were glass display cases filled with weapons and a wall of purses a woman could hide a dainty pistol in. This was a niche market I knew nothing about until I returned to Lisa's house later that day and went online. There I found websites selling gun-concealing vests, T-shirts, jackets—you name it. One company makes boxer briefs with a holster in the back, which they call "Compression Concealment Shorts" but which I would call gunderpants.

Lisa and I quite enjoyed wandering around the store. ROSSI R352—$349.77, read a tag beside one of the pistols. Were I in, say, an office-supply shop, I could have made a judgment concerning the cost, but I have no idea how much a gun goes for. It was like pricing penguins or milking equipment. My shooting experience was limited to air rifles. Lisa had no experience whatsoever, so before stepping onto the firing range we sat for a forty-minute gun-safety class taught by a retired Winston-Salem police officer named Lonnie, who co-owned the business and was dressed in one of its T-shirts. The man was perhaps in his early fifties, his pale eyebrows and wire-rimmed, almost invisible glasses shaded by a baseball cap with the Blackwater logo on it. He might not be someone you'd choose as a friend, but you wouldn't mind him as a neighbor. "I shoveled your drive while you were asleep," you could imagine him saying. "I hope you don't mind. I just wanted the exercise."

There was a classroom at the back of the store, and, after seating us side by side at one of the desks, Lonnie took the chair across from us. "The first thing you need to know about firearm safety is that most people are stupid. I don't mean you folks personally, but people in general. So I have a few rules. Number one: Always assume that every weapon is loaded."

Lisa and I leaned back, wincing, as he laid two guns in front of us. One was a Glock something, and the other—the nicer-looking one—was a snub-nosed .38 Special.

"Now, are these loaded?" he asked.

"I am going to assume that they are," Lisa answered.

Lonnie said, "Good girl."

I found a gun once while cleaning someone's apartment in New York. It was under the bed where the pornography should be, wrapped in a T-shirt, and it was in my lap before I realized what it was. Then I froze, the way I might have had it been a bomb. Eventually, very carefully, I nudged it back into place, wondering what the person who owned this looked like, for I had never met him.

I used to think that guys with beards had guns. Then I realized by asking around that guys with beards had *fathers* who owned guns. It was amazing how spot-on this was. I once met an Asian American fellow with a very sketchy goatee—no more than a dozen eyelash-length hairs on his chin—and when I guessed that his dad had bullets but no gun, he said, "Oh my God. How did you know?"

This was before beards came back into style and everyone grew one. Now I think that guys who wear baseball caps with their sunglasses perched on the brims have guns, if—and this is important—the lenses of those sunglasses are mirrored or fade from orange to yellow, like a tequila sunrise. As for women, I have no idea.

Lonnie had moved on by this point and was teaching us how to pick up our guns. Like most people raised on water pistols and dart-shooting plastic Lugers, we automatically reached for the triggers, a no-no in the Big Book of Safety. "These weapons absolutely cannot fire unless you tug that little piece of metal," Lonnie said.

"They can't go off if you drop them?" I asked.

"Absolutely not," he told me. "Almost never. So go on, David, pick up your Glock."

I screwed up my courage and did as instructed.

"Good job!"

When it was Lisa's turn, her finger went straight for the trigger.

"Busted," Lonnie told her. "OK, now, David, I want you to pick up the thirty-eight, and Lisa, you go for the Glock."

We'd just advanced to rule number two—never point your weapon at another person, unless you intend to kill or wound them—when Lisa explained why she was taking the class: "If anyone ever tries to shoot me? And accidentally drops the gun? I want to know how to handle it properly."

"That is a very good, very smart reason," Lonnie said. "I can tell you're someone who thinks ahead."

Oh, you have no *idea,* I thought.

Our safety session went a little over schedule but still allowed us ten minutes of shooting time, which, in retrospect, was more than enough. Seeing Lisa standing ramrod straight with a loaded Glock in her hand was as startling to me as seeing her in front of an orchestra waving a baton. Her first bullet hit the target—a life-sized outline of a man—and missed the bull's-eye of his heart by an inch at most.

Where did that come from? I wondered.

"Good girl!" Lonnie told her. "Now I want you to plant your legs a little farther apart and try again."

Her second shot was even closer.

"Lisa, you're a natural," Lonnie said. "OK, Mike, now you give it a try."

I looked around, confused. "Excuse me?"

He handed me the .38. "You came here to shoot, didn't you?"

I accepted the gun, and from then until the time we left, my name was Mike, which was more than a little demoralizing. Not getting the "Wait a minute—*the* David Sedaris?" I have come to expect when meeting someone was bad enough, but being turned into a *Mike*, of all things? I thought of the time a woman approached me in a hotel lobby. "Pardon me," she said, "but are you here for the Lions Club meeting?" That's the Mike of organizations.

Lonnie didn't forget my sister's name—on the contrary, he wore it out. "Good shot, Lisa! Now do it with your left eye closed." "What do you say, Lisa, ready to give the thirty-eight a try?"

"Do I have to?" she asked. The fact was that she was—that both of us were—already bored. Taking my final shot, I thought of a couple I know in Odessa, Texas. Tom repairs planes, so he and Randy live right there at the airport, in a prefabricated house beside the hangar he works out of. One night, late, a large, crazy-looking man who turned out to be an escaped mental patient drove through the high chain-link fence surrounding their property and pounded on their door. "I know you've got my mother in there!" he shouted. "I know you're holding her hostage, you bastard!"

It was absurd, the things he was saying, but there was no dissuading him.

Tom and Randy were on the other side of the door, bolstering it with their bodies, and when it started to come off its hinges, Tom ran for his pistol.

"You have a *gun?*" I asked, surprised, I suppose, because he's gay.

Tom nodded. "I fired at where I thought his knees would be, but he was bent over at the time, so the bullet went into his neck."

It didn't kill him, though. Enraged, the escaped mental patient got back behind the wheel and drove through the massive garage-style door of the hangar. Then it was out through the back wall and onto the tarmac, where he made a U-turn and drove into Tom and Randy's house.

"Wait," I said. "This is like a movie where the villain refuses to die."

"I know!" agreed Randy, who directs his local arts council. "I'm the pacifist in this relationship, never held a gun in my life, but there I was while this madman was driving past my chest of drawers, shouting, 'Kill him!'"

As Tom aimed his gun again, the guy passed out from blood loss, and not long afterward the police showed up. By then, the door was hanging by a thread and had bullet holes in it, the hangar was practically destroyed, and there was a stolen car at the foot of their bed. *This,* I thought, *is exactly why people buy guns.* The NRA could have used their story as a commercial.

Who would I want to shoot? I asked myself, looking at the silhouette in front of me and wondering if there was also a female version. Of course, it wouldn't have mattered who I imagined killing. The bullet I fired was so off the mark, my only hope was that my enemy would laugh themselves to death.

*   *   *

At the end of our session, Lonnie pulled in our target and wrote Lisa's name above the bullet hole that came closest to the heart. Above the one that was farthest away, he wrote, "Mike." Then he rolled it up and handed it to us as a souvenir. Later, as I paid, Lonnie said that North Carolina had pretty good laws. "We're a very gun-friendly state," he said.

I told him that in England a man was sent to prison for shooting a burglar who was breaking into his home, and Lonnie's jaw dropped. It was as if I'd said that where I live, you have to walk on your hands between the hours of six a.m. and noon. "Now, that's just crazy," he said. Turning to the fellow next to him, he asked, "Did you hear that?" Then he turned back to me. "I'm telling you, Mike, sometimes I don't know what this world is coming to."

In the glass case below the counter were a number of bumper stickers, one of which read, PROSHOTS: PANSIES CONVERTED DAILY.

"That used to be on their billboard until gay people complained," Lisa told me as we walked out the door.

I'm not a person who is easily offended. There's a lot I don't like in this world. There's plenty of stuff that makes me *angry,* but the only things I can think of that really offend me, that truly affront my sense of decency, are cartoons in which animals wear sunglasses and say "awesome" all the time. That, to me, is crossing the line. It's not because the animal in question—some rabbit or bear or whatever—is being disrespected but because it's training children to be mediocre. Calling gay people pansies is just "meh," in my opinion.

"What was that 'reason for taking the class' business all about?" I asked Lisa as we crossed the parking lot to her car. "What makes you think that your attacker is going to drop his gun?"

She unlocked her door and opened it. "I don't know. Maybe he'll be wearing gloves and lose his grip."

As we pulled away, I wondered if depressed people ever took the safety class and turned the guns on themselves once they got on the firing range. "It would be more practical than buying your own Glock or thity-eight, and there'd be no mess," I said. "At least not in your home. And, seeing as how you don't pay until the *end* of the session, it wouldn't cost you anything. Except, you know, your life."

Lisa considered this. "I always thought that before I committed suicide, I'd first kill Henry." She was referring to her parrot, who could easily live to be seventy. "Don't get me wrong, I love him to death. I just don't want him to be abused once I'm gone."

"I thought he went to me after you died," I said.

Lisa signaled for a turn. "You'd just lose interest in him."

Not long after we took our safety class, Sandy Hook happened. Two months after that, ProShots emailed a Valentine greeting. It was a photo of a heart shape made of weapons. There were pistols and semiautomatic rifles. Even hand grenades. I read that, after the shooting, gun sales went up, the fear being that

President Obama was going to repeal the Second Amendment. The same thing happened after that guy opened fire in a movie theater in Colorado, and after the massacre at the Emanuel African Methodist Episcopal Church in South Carolina.

It's so foreign to me, wanting to own a gun, especially the kind you'd use in a war. I don't know why, but shooting just doesn't appeal to me. I tried it that one time with Lisa and don't feel the need to ever do it again. People on YouTube blow away bowling pins and old toaster ovens in their backyards, and I just don't get it. I've never thought to stalk and kill my own food. I don't worry that a race war is coming and I need to arm myself in advance of it. Nor am I concerned that an escaped psychopath is going to break down my front door in the middle of the night. Things like that clearly happen, but I'd just as soon prepare by having a back door. Where I live now, in the UK, it's hard to get a rifle and next to impossible to secure a handgun. Yet somehow, against all odds, British people feel free. Is it that they don't know what they're missing? Or is the freedom they feel the freedom of not being shot to death in a classroom or shopping mall or movie theater?

Of course, UK stabbings are through the roof, but with a knife you're not going to kill more than a few people at a time. Then too there's not a movement built around bladed weapons the way there is around firearms. I've yet to see a bumper sticker picturing a fencing sword and the words COME AND TAKE IT or THINK TWICE. BECAUSE I WON'T. A few days after Sandy Hook, I went online and saw an ad for the Bushmaster, one of the weapons used by Adam Lanza. It was a picture of the assault rifle above the words CONSIDER YOUR MAN CARD REISSUED.

Every school shooting is different but the same. We see the news footage, the crying children, the flowers and teddy bears in a pile getting rained on. There are reports that the community is "healing," and then it's on to the next one. The solution, according to the NRA, is for more people to have guns. When President Trump—following the mass murder in Parkland, Florida—proposed arming teachers, I called Lisa, who sounded skeptical. "Wait a second," she said. "Where did you read this?"

I thought of a dinner a few years earlier. My sister had joined me for a weekend in Chicago and asked my friend Adam, "Are you familiar with a newspaper called *The Onion*?"

"Of course," he said.

"I didn't know what it was, see? Then I read an article claiming that, in order to save money, schools in America were going to eliminate the past tense. After I finished it, I phoned my husband and told him, 'This is the last straw.' Because I used to teach, and the way budgets are being cut nowadays, this seemed entirely possible to me."

"How do you save money by eliminating the past tense?" Adam asked.

"I don't know," Lisa said. "I guess I wasn't thinking clearly."

It's probably for the best that someone so gullible is no longer in front of a classroom. Still, I can't blame her for not believing the armed-teacher business. Who'd have thought that after all was said and done this would be the proposed solution? A few days later, the Blue Mountain School District in eastern Pennsylvania put buckets of river rocks in all its classrooms, the idea being for the kids to stone their would-be assassins.

I think there might be a few who'd reach for a rock, but wouldn't most of them freeze or just start crying? I know I would.

Then came Santa Fe, Texas, where to my family's great shame the shooter was named Dimitrios Pagourtzis.

We felt the way Korean Americans likely did after Virginia Tech.

"Oh no," we said. "He's one of us!"

Luckily the state's lieutenant governor was casting blame on the number of exits and entrances the building had rather than on, say, Greece. "The school that I taught at is now holding active-shooter drills," Lisa told me. "That's where the students—and mine were third graders—turn off the lights and hide in dark corners." She sighed. "I'm just glad I got out when I did."

When my sister and I were young, during the Cuban missile crisis, we had atomic-bomb drills. You'd think our teachers would have led us to shelters twelve stories underground, but instead we were told to crouch beneath our desks. What were we thinking, kneeling there with our hands atop our heads? Did we believe the bombs might, at the very most, blow off a few ceiling tiles and that after the attack we'd return to our homes and find everything just as we had left it? Our parents, our pets, dinner waiting with maybe a little dust on it?

Being shot is easier for children to wrap their heads around. If you've got a TV in your house, you know what a gun is and what happens to people when they're hit with bullets. You may not have a clear concept of death—its permanence, its refusal to be bargained with—but you know it's bad. For us at the time, with Lisa in the second grade and me in the first, the atomic bomb was just an abstraction. So when I'd see my sister on the school bus at the end of a drill day—in a dress and patent-leather shoes, her hair just so, looking far more elegant than she ever would as an adult—I wouldn't feel relieved so much as excited, the way kids that age are when they're released into the world at the end of the day. Oh, to be alive, and free.

Father Time

The night before his ninety-fifth birthday party, my father fell while turning around in his kitchen. My sister Lisa and her husband, Bob, dropped by hours later to hook up his new TV and discovered him on the floor, disoriented and in pain. He fell again after they righted him, so an ambulance was called. At the hospital, they met up with our sister Gretchen and with Amy, who'd just flown in from New York to attend the party, which was now canceled. "It was really weird," she said when we spoke on the phone the following morning. "Dad thought Lisa was Mom, and when the doctor asked him where he was, he answered, 'Syracuse'—where he went to college. Then he got mad and said, 'You're sure asking a lot of questions.' As if that's not normal for a doctor. I think he thought this was just *some guy* he was talking to."

Fortunately, he was lucid again by the following afternoon.

That was the hard part for everyone—seeing him so confused.

On the night that my father fell, I was in Princeton, New Jersey, the fourth of eighty cities I would be traveling to for work. On the morning he was moved from the hospital to a rehabilitation center, I was on my way to Ann Arbor. Over the next week, he had a few little strokes, the sort people don't notice right away. One affected his peripheral vision, and another, his short-term memory. He'd wanted to return home after leaving rehab, but by this point there was no way he could continue to live alone.

I'm not sure where I was when my father moved into his assisted living center. Springmoor, it's called. I saw it, finally, four months after his fall, when Hugh and I flew to North Carolina. It was early August, and we arrived to find him in an easy chair, blood flowing from his ear at what seemed to me a pretty alarming rate. It looked fake, like beet juice, and was being dabbed at by a nurse's assistant. "Oh, hello," my father said, his voice soft and weary-sounding.

I thought he didn't know who I was, but then he added my name and held out his hand. "David." He looked behind me. "Hugh." Someone had wrapped his head with gauze, and when he leaned back he resembled the late English poet Edith Sitwell, very distinguished-looking, almost imperious. His eyebrows were thin and barely perceptible. It was the same with his lashes. I guess that, like the hairs on his arms and legs, they just got tired of holding on.

"So what happened?" I asked, though I already knew.

Lisa had told me that morning on the phone that the grand-father clock he'd brought to Springmoor had fallen on him. It was made of walnut and bronze and had an abstract human face on it, surrounded by numbers that were tilted at odd angles. My mother always referred to it as Mr. Creech, after the artist who made it, but my dad calls it Father Time.

I'd said to Hugh after hanging up with Lisa, "When you're ninety-five, and Father Time *literally* knocks you to the ground, don't you think he's maybe trying to tell you something?"

"He insisted on moving it himself," the woman attempting to stanch the bleeding said, "and it cut his ear. We sent him to the hospital for stitches, but now it's started up again, maybe because he's on blood thinners, so we've called an ambulance." She turned to my father and raised her voice. *"Haven't we, Lou? Haven't we called an ambulance?!"*

At that moment, two EMTs bounded in, both young and bearded, like lumberjacks. Each took an elbow and helped my father to stand.

"Are we going somewhere?" he asked.

"Back to the hospital!" the woman shouted.

"All right," my father said. "OK."

They wheeled him out, and the woman explained that, while the staff would remove bloodstains from the carpet, it was the family's job to get them off any privately owned furniture. "I can bring you some towels," she suggested.

A few moments later, another aide walked into the room. "Excuse me," she said, "but are you the famous son?"

"I'm a pretty sorry excuse for famous," I told her. "But yes, I'm his son."

"So you're Dave? Dave Chappelle? Can I have your autograph? Actually, can I have two?"

"Um, sure," I said.

I'd just joined Hugh in cleaning the easy chair when the woman, who seemed slightly nervous, the way you might be around a world-famous comedian who is young and Black and has his whole life ahead of him, returned for two more autographs.

"I'm the worst son in the world," I told her, reaching for the scraps of paper she was holding out. "My father fell on April seventh, and this is the first time I've visited, the first time I've *talked* to him, even."

"You put yourself down too much," the woman said. "Just pick up the phone every so often—that's what I do with my mother." She offered a forgiving smile. "You can make that second autograph to my supervisor." And she gave me a name.

The blood on our wet rags looked even faker than the blood I'd watched falling from my father's ear. I took a few half-hearted swipes at the easy chair, but it was Hugh who did most of the work. Mainly I looked at the things my dad had decorated his room with: Father Time, a number of the streetscapes he and my mother bought in the seventies, rocks he'd carried back from fishing trips, each with a date and the name of the river it had come from written on it. All of it was so depressing to me. Then again, even a unicorn would have looked dingy in this place. I don't know if it was the lighting, or the height of the ceiling. Perhaps it was the hospital bed against the wall, or the floor-length curtains that looked as if they'd come from a funeral parlor. Down the hall, a dozen or so residents, most in wheelchairs and some drooling onto bibs, were watching *M*A*S*H* on television.

I couldn't help but think of Mayview, the nursing home my father put his mother in, back in the midseventies. It seemed like only yesterday that I'd gone with him to see her. If now here *I* was, visiting him in a similar place, wouldn't it be me, in the blink of an eye, in my own assisted living center, *me* the frail widower reduced to a single room? Only I won't have children to look after me, the way my father had Lisa—who had been extraordinary—and my brother, Paul, and Amy and Gretchen. My sister-in-law, Kathy, had outdone everyone, stopping by sometimes twice a day, taking Dad to lunch, rubbing lotion into his feet. I was the only exception. Me. Dave Chappelle.

"Do you think we can get a few pictures together?" one of the nurses asked me on my way out.

"Oh, wait, I want one too," another woman said, and another after her.

"Look," I imagined them telling people afterward, "I got a photo of me with Dave Chappelle."

"No, you didn't," they'd be told.

Of course, I'd be long gone by then. Like always.

Hugh and I drove to our house on Emerald Isle—the Sea Section—after leaving Springmoor, and were joined a few days later by his older brother, John, who'd brought two boys: his seven-year-old grandson, Harrison, and Harrison's half brother, Austin, who was eleven. All three live in a small town on a strait several hours west of Seattle. The kids had never encountered water they could walk into without shrieking from the cold. They'd never seen fine sand or pelicans. I thought they'd be thrilled, but it was hard luring them away from the portable gaming console they'd brought from Washington—a Nintendo Switch.

"What?" Harrison cried, exasperated, after touring the house. "You don't have a TV we can hook this up to?"

He was one of those children who'd skipped cute and gone straight to handsome. I supposed this could change over the next few decades: His nose might grow out of proportion to the rest of his face. He could lose his chin or a cheek in some sort of accident, but even then he'd have his eyes, which were cornflower blue, and a pouty, almost feminine mouth, the lower lip slightly larger than the top one. Everywhere we went, he was the best-looking person in the room. *Does he realize it?* I wondered. Kids his age are usually oblivious.

Looks aside, Harrison and his half brother, both of whom live with their mother, were far from spoiled. The Nintendo was something John had given them earlier that year. They aren't allowed one at home, and after a few hours I could understand why. The console was the first thing they'd reach for in the morning and the last thing they'd look at before going to bed, which most nights was well after one a.m.

The boys didn't seem to have any rules the way I did when

I was their age. "You can't just leave the table," I said to Harrison on the first night of his visit, when he finished his dinner and ran off to play Minecraft. "You have to ask if you can be excused."

"No, I don't."

"No, I don't, *Mr. Sedaris*." I made the boys call me that, and would correct them whenever they slipped up. "I'm an adult and you're guests in *my* house."

"It's not your house, it's *Hugh's*," Harrison said.

Hugh looked up from his plate. "He's right. Look at the deed. This place is in my name."

"Yes, well, *I* bought it," I said.

Harrison rolled his eyes. "Yeah, right."

The following afternoon I came down from my desk and found him and his half brother on the sofa, gaming again.

"Why don't you put the Nintendo away and write a letter to your mother?" I said.

Harrison nudged Austin in the ribs: "Stranger danger." This, apparently, was something they'd learned in school. "Don't talk to him."

"I'm not a stranger, I'm your host, and it wouldn't hurt you to be a little more like me for a change."

"What's so good about you?" Harrison asked.

"Two things," I said, my mind racing as I tried to think of something. "I'm rich and I'm famous."

He shook his head, eyes locked on his game. "I don't believe a word you say."

"Hugh!" I called. "Will you tell Harrison I'm rich and famous?"

"I think he's out on the beach," Austin said, his eyes glued, like his half brother's, on the paperback-sized console they were sharing. "What did you do to get famous?"

"Wrote books," I said.

"Well, I never heard of any of them," Harrison told me.

"That's because you're *seven,*" I said, more hurt than I care to admit. "Grown-ups know who I am. Especially nurses."

Later that afternoon, for the fourth time that week, Hugh saw someone taking pictures of our house. "I think they read your last book," he said.

"See!" I shouted to Harrison in the next room.

He was into his game and didn't answer.

"They're most likely just taking pictures of the Sea Section sign," I said to Hugh. "It *is* a pretty good name for a beach house." I then told him about a place our neighbor Bermey had mentioned that was farther up the coast and was called YOU DIDN'T GET THIS, BITCH. "That probably gets photographed as well," I said, "especially by divorced men."

The picture-taking on the street side of our house was nothing compared to what was going on out back. When I was young, sea turtles would lay their eggs on the beach, and no one thought much about it. Now, though, it's a huge deal. Loggerheads are on bumper stickers and signs. They're an attraction, like the wild horses near Ocracoke. The spot where the eggs are laid is marked, and when the time arrives for them to hatch, a team of volunteers from the Turtle Patrol is dispatched.

A bright-yellow stake had been driven into the sand near the foot of the wooden staircase that led from our house to the beach, and, the morning after the boys arrived, volunteers dug a trench that would make it easier for the hatchlings to find the ocean. Now it was lined on either side with folding chairs, and the Turtle Patrol nest-sitting. I said to Hugh, "It's like the red carpet at the Academy Awards."

People walking down the beach, seeing the yellow caution tape and the trench monitored by do-gooders in bright Turtle Patrol T-shirts, wandered over to ask questions, and the crowd grew. At night, they'd sit with infrared flashlights, intently staring down, watching for the slightest movement, with their cameras at the ready.

"It's actually called a *boil*," Kathy told me. "That's because when the eggs hatch and the babies claw their way to the surface, the sand churns."

"Isn't that exciting?" I said to the boys.

"Uh-huh," they answered. "Sure."

"Really?" I said. "You're not interested in nature?" When I was their age it was pretty much all I cared about—that and stealing and spying on people. I told them about the hideous-looking silver possum who'd climbed up the front stairs of the house last Thanksgiving. "We fed her fruit and leftovers, and you should have seen the way her hands grabbed the food, almost like a human. Every night she came."

Austin politely but vacantly said, "Wow."

The only way to get the boys' attention was by throwing one of the stink bombs I'd bought a week earlier, on Cape Cod. I'd thought the smell would be negligible—maybe like an old sock—but instead it cleared not just the room where the boys were playing Mario Kart but an entire side of the house. It was sulfur, for the most part, what I imagine Satan's bathroom would smell like after he'd been on the toilet with the *National Review* for a while.

"Goddammit," Hugh said, holding his nose and opening the front and back doors, letting the hot, humid air in. "And we have company coming!"

"Why you...book writer," Harrison scolded. He was wearing Minecraft pajamas and looked like a male model who'd been put into a machine and made small.

Of the two brothers, Austin had the sweeter temperament. He'd ask questions and offer to help out. His voice had an old-fashioned quality to it, like a boy's in a radio serial. "Gee willikers!" you could imagine him saying, if that were the name of a video game in which things blew up and women got shot in the back of the head.

Compared to other kids I've known, the two were actually pretty good. Both liked fish, and they always ate everything on their plates. Rarely did they bicker, and when they did it was over within a minute or two. There was no crying, and, better still, no sulking. That, to me, is unbearable. "Oh, move on, for God's sake," my mother used to say when we glared and stewed, vowing to never forget the injustice of egg salad, or potato chips that were from the bottom of the bag, and broken.

The boys weren't terribly interested in the boil taking place in the back of the house, but I thought they might change their minds if they saw the baby loggerheads. The eggs were the size of Ping-Pong balls and were supposed to hatch on Monday. Then Tuesday. Then Wednesday. At night, we'd walk to the top of our stairway and see if there was any action. "Aren't we lucky to have a front-row seat!" I'd say.

"If you say so," Harrison would answer.

My fifteen-year-old niece, Maddy, had the same attitude. She was at the beach as well, though you'd hardly know it. We'd see her briefly at lunch and dinner, but the rest of her time was spent in seclusion, her face six inches from her phone. *Was there an equivalent when I was young?* I wondered. I don't recall my parents crying, "You and that goddamn transistor radio!"

The boys slept in what we'd come to think of as my father's room. It was strange being at the beach without him, but we didn't yet have the proper equipment: a walk-in shower, bars beside the toilet, and so on. A year earlier, he hadn't needed those things, but that's the difference between ninety-four and ninety-five. The day before his fall, he'd driven to the gym, not knowing that it would be his last time behind the wheel of a car, his last night in his own bed. There would be a lot of that in his immediate future: the last time he could dress himself, the last time he could walk.

I worried that he had entered a period when it would be one

thing after another, death by a thousand cuts: a fall, a stroke, an accident with a grandfather clock. That's how it was with the other extremely old people I've known in my life: the woman across the road from us in Normandy, our next-door neighbor in London. Phyllis Diller. Late in her life, the two of us became friends. She lived in a mansion in Brentwood, and each time I'd visit her there, she'd be a bit less able—her eyes wouldn't stop watering or she couldn't get up from a chair. Phyllis was lucky in that she could remain at home and hire round-the-clock help; lucky too that she was famous—a legend by any definition. All day, disciples came to pay homage to her, and every night she went out. Thus she was spared the loneliness so many old people have to suffer.

The last time I went to her house, I found her on the back patio. It was one in the afternoon and she was drinking a martini. "Karla," she called to her assistant, "get David here something to drink. What would you like, sweetie, a vodka?"

"Just some water," I said, settling in beside her.

"Water with vodka in it?"

"No, just the water."

"Bring him a vodka tonic," Phyllis instructed, forgetting, I guess, that I don't drink.

In Karla's absence, she pointed to two pigeons parading across her beautifully landscaped lawn. "All those two do," she said, lifting her glass with her blue-veined hand, the fingers as thin and brittle as twigs, "I mean *all* they do, is fuck."

*　　*　　*

We were off somewhere when most of the turtles hatched, some sixty-three of them. We missed the six that clawed their way out early the following morning as well. Hugh's brother left with the boys on a Sunday, and a few hours later the final one burst forth. I was on a walk when it happened, and returned minutes after it had stumbled down the trench and into the ocean. "It was heartbreaking," Hugh reported. He was standing in his bathing suit on the beach behind our house, one in a crowd of fifty or so.

"What was so sad?" I asked. "I mean, he made it, right?"

Hugh's voice cracked. "Yes but...he was just so...alone."

"I can't believe you missed it," he said as we were going to bed that night. He'd just pulled his shirt off, and I took a moment to admire his tan. It was nothing he'd worked for; rather, it just came, the result of all the hours he'd spent in the ocean, occasionally with the boys but mainly on his own, swimming like some sort of creature, one moment on his back and the next on his stomach, turning like a chicken on a spit. He's done this since childhood, and as a result his shoulders are so broad I can barely get my arms around them. Still I try. He slips beneath the covers and I cleave to him like a barnacle, thinking of all the couples I know who no longer share a bed. "He snores!" the wife will tell me, or "I need my own space." I'd hate separate rooms, though a sleep-apnea machine might be a deal breaker, or incontinence. Definitely incontinence. I can't predict what's waiting for us, lurking on the other side of our late middle age, but I know it can't be good.

Before returning to England, we drove back to Raleigh and ate lunch with my father, who had a biscuit-sized bandage on his ear and was relying on a walker that had his name and room number written on it in Magic Marker. I didn't want to meet at Springmoor—"You told us you were Dave Chappelle!"—so Lisa and Bob drove him to a café we'd all agreed on. Watching from a distance as he slowly advanced toward the table, I was struck by how breakable he seemed. Still, his spirits were high, and he was engaging, funny even, especially when talking about Springmoor and the way the staff will walk in whenever they want to: "It's a problem because I don't always feel like wearing clothes, if you catch my drift."

"Sure," I said, thinking, *What's wrong with underpants at least?*

Kathy met us at the restaurant as well, and midway through our meal she told my father about the baby loggerheads she'd seen hatching a few days earlier on Emerald Isle.

"Oh, right," my father said. "They've laid their eggs there for centuries. For even longer, I imagine. Eons."

"And the last one to pop up out of the sand," she reported, "the very last one, the Turtle Patrol people named Lou. Isn't that something!"

A more sentimental audience might have moved their hands to their hearts and cooed. Eyes might have misted or filled with actual tears. Had someone named a human baby after my father—called it, say, Lou Sedaris Kwitchoff, or, better yet, Louis Harry Sedaris Kwitchoff—my family might have shared a moment over our salads and sandwiches there at the Belted Goat. But this was an endangered turtle with only a tiny chance of living until the end of the week, and so it was more like naming a bar of soap after someone, if soap could paddle around briefly.

"What can I tell you?" my father said, his voice soft and dry, like corn husks being rubbed together. "I'm notorious. I'm legendary. I'm a survivor."

Bruised

When Hugh was in his late twenties, he bought an old stone farmhouse in a small village in Normandy. It didn't cost much, but it didn't have much either: no electricity or running water, a roof that needed replacing. He took offense when I called it a dump, so instead I referred to it as a hovel, which I think it technically was. The floor on the ground level was hard-packed dirt. On the second level it was wood, but worm-eaten, and it was the same in the attic. All of the beams were rotted as well, as were the doors and windows. The previous owner had left an armoire, a table, and half a dozen barrels, several of which were big enough for me to stand in. Upstairs and down, the place smelled like old rope.

I first saw the hovel in 1992, a couple of years after Hugh and I met. I knew no French back then, other than a few odd words I'd picked up: *traffic jam, raw,* the verb *to shorten,* for some reason. And then, of course, all the English words that just happen to be French: *Nocturnal. Surveillance. Cliché.* I assumed that the villagers would have learned a little something from watching American TV. *Dallas* was still huge at the time. People were naming their daughters Pamela, but that was as far as they were willing to go back then. So, on my first four visits, I spent all my time smiling and trying to look as though I knew what was going on.

It was so humbling, being robbed of my personality like that. I was never the smartest guy in the room, but I could usually hold my own. In Normandy, though, I was considered an idiot. Worse still, I couldn't get a laugh to save my life. In America that was my thing, my identity. I was on the radio and in magazines. Now I was just a lump, and it was Hugh who commanded all the attention. He spoke and understood French perfectly but couldn't really be counted on to translate, especially if there were a lot of people around. Once we got electricity and water, he started inviting friends over. Groups of ten would arrive for lunch, and I'd feel so left out. "What did she say?" I once asked after a guest had held the floor for a few minutes, then hidden her face in her hands.

"She vomited on herself at her wedding. I'll tell you later."

I hated being excluded, so between a brief visit in May 1997 and a much longer one the following August, I took a ten-session private French class taught by a petite, sharp-nosed thumbtack of a woman. Elise was Canadian, and we met twice a week in the World Trade Center. At around the same time, I started opening my Larousse dictionary, writing random nouns on index cards, and memorizing them on my daily walks. "Why did you learn the word *bruise*?" she groused one afternoon. "When is *that* going to come in handy?"

In retrospect, I suppose I can see her point. Why master *bruise* before, say, *umbrella*? How many of us know, though, when learning a foreign language, what words and phrases might prove useful? It's like predicting the future.

If I had it to do over, I'd perfect the line "Let us go see what your grandmother is up to," though *bruise* came in handy as well that summer. Hugh and I had the main support beam in the living room replaced, which was a massive undertaking. While we were treating the new one for worms, I fell off my ladder and bashed my thigh against a heavy chair. "Look," I said the following morning, pointing to the purple smudge on my skin, "a bruise!"

I repeated it later that day to the woman across the road. Madame G was impressed but still corrected my pronunciation. "Ecchy*mose*," she said. "Pas ecchy*muse*." She and her husband were in their early seventies at the time and raised horses and sheep. They kept chickens as well, and rabbits. In the doll-sized house right next to theirs, they kept Madame G's active, ninety-eight-year-old mother, Granny G, who had long white hair and took walks through the forest every afternoon, collecting either berries or mushrooms, depending on the season. They also took care of Monsieur G's younger sister, Clotilde, who had Down syndrome and was very short. People with her condition sometimes die fairly young, but she was in her midfifties. Clotilde wore thick glasses that made her eyes appear small. She had gray hair and whiskers, and spent her days standing up dominoes, then knocking them over. When the weather was good she did it on a metal-topped table in her front yard, stopping only when Madame G barked, *"Monte!"* This was her cue to climb the front stairs to the house, and then another set to the second floor, where the bathroom was. She would sit on the toilet until the end of time unless someone instructed her to get off it, Madame G explained to Hugh, though not impatiently. She had great affection for her sister-in-law.

The only word I ever heard Clotilde say was *big*, this in French, of course, and in response to a question that was always the same: "Do you want a big slice of tart or a small one?"

"Gros," Clotilde would moan, and everyone would applaud.

"Everyone" that summer often included Madame and Monsieur G's two grown children and six grandchildren. Three belonged to their son, who worked for the electric company and had a number of crudely rendered tattoos on his arms. Then there were three boys born to their daughter. The middle one was twelve and named Olivier. I'd first met him a year earlier, but he'd gotten taller since then, and now had two inches on me. Between one August and the next, he had grown furtive in the same way I had when I was his age. I gathered he had come into possession of a secret—that he was gay. It's funny how that works. One moment you're a child and know only that there's something different about you, something that separates you from other boys. Then you get a little older and understand what that thing is.

If you attend a progressive private school and have supportive parents who've got lots of artistic friends, maybe you can go straight from your realization to acceptance. Olivier's family seemed pretty cool. His grandparents had no problem with me and Hugh, or with the lesbian couple who would later move in down the road and were so butch that at first we all took them to be men. But twelve is young, especially in those pre-internet days, and more so when you lived, as Olivier did, in a town of only thirteen thousand.

In our tiny village the population was closer to fifty, and most everyone was either retired or well into adulthood. There was no one for the kids to hang out with except one another and the inarticulate man-child—me—who lived just across the road. I was over at the Gs' a lot that summer, hoping to improve my French. At first I understood nothing. Then a single word, then two. *"Viens...Intermarché?"* one of the Gs would ask. I'd get into their car and ride with them to the charmless Walmart-style hypermarket they liked to shop at. It was the sort of place that sold both scallions *and* riding lawn mowers, the sort that smelled like a brand-new beach ball and was killing small businesses all across the country. "Why here?" I wanted to ask, though the answer was obvious. There was no real money to be made raising sheep. The hypermarkets sold things more cheaply and in bulk.

The grandkids were around a lot that August, especially Olivier and his cousin Claudette, who would grow up to become a nurse. One night we gathered in the Gs' cramped dining room to celebrate her thirteenth birthday, and when the lights were turned off in advance of the candle-lit cake, I cried, in a panicked, accusatory voice, *"Mon portefeuille!"* (*My wallet!*) and got my very first laugh in French.

"Take children...river?" Madame G proposed the following afternoon.

It wasn't far from her house, a ten-minute walk across a pasture and through the woods. Claudette and Olivier talked to each other along the way. I heard the words *beach... hot...Spain.* That was where Olivier and his family had recently returned from, all of them deeply tanned. They were nice-looking boys, beautiful, really, all with their mother's black hair and olive complexion. At fifteen, the oldest was already handsome. His features had settled while Olivier's were still in play, the eyes a bit too large. They made his mouth appear small and girlish. It was a doll's face, flecked with moles that reminded me of my own when I was his age.

I noticed once we entered the woods that Olivier kept tripping and grabbing on to me for support. The first two times it happened, I didn't give it much thought. Then I realized it was an act, an excuse to make physical contact. He did the same as we crossed the river. The water was cool and shallow, easy to traverse on large flat rocks spaced no more than a foot apart. A child half Olivier's age could have done it, but he kept pretending to lose his balance. Then he'd grab hold of me in places that seemed strategic: my stomach, my butt, my upper arms. His hands lingered, feeling me rather than just relying on me for support.

"Look!" he said at one point. I turned toward him, and he pulled down his swimsuit, pointing to what looked like a mosquito bite on his bottom.

His cousin laughed, and I thought, *No, put that away!*

A moment later I saw Granny G coming down the path with a basket of blackberries. *"Bonjour!"* I called, in a way that meant *Help!*—and so loudly that birds took flight.

I noticed that when we returned to the Gs' house, Olivier lowered his eyes and refused to look at me. There was no change in Claudette's behavior. She was her same, cheerful self, but for her cousin, once there were other adults around, I was dead to him.

I said to Hugh over dinner that night, "Can a person be sexually harassed by a twelve-year-old?"

The following afternoon I was at home, writing in the milking parlor I used as an office, when Olivier let himself in the back door. "Hugh...here?"

I said no, and he hopped up the short staircase to our bedroom. "You two...together?" he asked. At least that's what I thought he was getting at. To make it clear he turned his hands into fists and bumped one against the other. I was trying to determine how to answer when he threw his arms around me. The kiss he planted would have met my lips had I not turned my head as fast as I did, causing it to land instead just above my left ear. It was so unexpected—shocking, really. In the same moment I considered how this would appear were someone to look in through the window, and I wriggled away, saying, "Grandmother!" When Olivier grabbed me again, my mind turned to those old *New Yorker* cartoons: the boss chasing his secretary around the desk. But in reverse. With the secretary being male as well. And a child.

When I recounted this story to a friend back in New York, he wondered why I hadn't been firmer. "Why not say, 'Look, this is inappropriate'?"

I explained that, grammatically speaking, the sentence—and the delicate ones it would lead to—was beyond me. Then too I remembered what it was like to be twelve and gay. You might grope a boy your age at a slumber party, pretending you were just horsing around, but if he called you on it, you'd deny everything and then set out to destroy him. "Me? It was *you* who started it!" The shame, the guilt—it's overwhelming when you're a kid.

Were I to embarrass Olivier, he could have said anything. And who would people in the village believe? The cute twelve-year-old with the nice family, or the foreigner who talks like a baby and is a known homosexual?

"Grandmother!" I repeated, racing out the front door, which we always kept open. Everyone's was, regardless of the flies it let in. A closed front door meant that you were either asleep or up to something.

Olivier had no interest in Hugh, just me, for some reason. Perhaps because I'm small and was closer to his size. Then too I've never had any authority. Not even first graders do what I tell them to do. I thought this might change as I grew older, but it hasn't. Nobody is afraid of me.

I'm guessing Olivier watched the house, waiting until Hugh's car left and he knew I was alone, for he never came over otherwise. I took to closing and locking the front door, but that didn't stop him from crawling through the window one afternoon. I was taking a nap, and when I awoke to find him standing beside the bed, I knew I was in for it. "Grandmother!" I cried. But before I could stand, he was down on the mattress, practically in my lap, his heart beating so loudly I could hear both it and Clotilde's dominoes falling against the metal-topped table across the road.

I said to Hugh that night, "What surprises me is his brazenness. I'd never have been so bold when I was twelve, even if the other person was my age." I wondered whether Olivier had had an experience with a teacher or a coach, or maybe just some gay grown-up he'd run into. I was forty-one that summer. That was ancient to a seventh grader, but again, I could understand what he might have been going through. When I was his age I used to wait until everyone else in my house was asleep. Then I'd creep into the family room, where my father would be conked out in front of the TV. He'd be in his underpants, like always, snoring in his chair, and I'd sit on the coffee table, studying him. Most often I'd be wearing a pair of briefs I'd cut the back out of with scissors. It's nothing I'm proud of, just the opposite. Recalling it fills me with shame. Even at the time I wondered, *What on earth am I doing?* I don't know what I thought would have happened were my father to wake up. It wasn't sex I wanted. I'm not sure I understood the mechanics of it then, the what-went-where part. I suppose I just wanted to cuddle. With my dad. Wearing underpants I'd cut the back out of. And my brown-framed glasses.

Our family room was on the ground floor and always smelled of mildew. It was accessible from the outside by way of two sliding glass doors, and more than once I wondered what someone looking in might have thought. It didn't last long, this phase, a couple of months, maybe. And I didn't do it every night. The following afternoon I'd watch my sisters eating their cookies or potato chips off the coffee table I'd sat on with my bare bottom and feel so ashamed of myself. I was out of control that year, completely. And so too, I knew, was Olivier.

I half considered going to his grandparents, with Hugh in tow to translate. But when you're a gay kid, your greatest fear is that someone's going to rat you out. I couldn't in good conscience do that. And again, were Olivier to feel cornered, he might say anything. When I was eleven—a year younger than he was—I developed a crush on a neighborhood woman named Mrs. Haugh. I don't recall why I chose her over any other mother on our street. She had a nice laugh, I remember, and was always kind to me, asking questions and seeming to really listen to my answers. Mrs. Haugh was plump and had three or maybe four children. I started by leaving flowers outside her kitchen door, then homemade cards. I'd creep over early and wait until her husband—my rival—left for work. One morning I went with a fresh bouquet and found an envelope waiting for me. In it was a note that read:

Dear David,

If I were ever to fall in love again, it would be with you.

All these years later I can still admire what a perfect response that was: This is never going to happen, but thanks so much for noticing me.

Would the same message have worked with Olivier? The difference, I suppose, was that all I'd done with Mrs. Haugh was leave flowers. Then too she was a respectable mother. Me having a crush on her—it was cute, a joke, something the grown-ups on my street could laugh about. A gay man, on the other hand, couldn't risk putting the word *love* in a note to a twelve-year-old boy.

Olivier came around a few more times before his school year began and he stopped spending days in our village. It was always the same: he'd creep in and, grabbing my cigarettes off the desk because I knew I wouldn't be back for a while, I'd say, "Grandmother!" Then I'd rush across the road to the Gs' house and he'd reluctantly follow me, sulking until Hugh returned and I could go back to work.

In early September I flew home to New York, where I could talk and be recognized as a whole person. I didn't see Olivier again until the following August. By that time my French had improved, and he had outgrown me. "This kid's going to be a famous fashion designer," Madame G announced, beaming in his direction as we sat around her living room one afternoon. "He's even taking sewing lessons, aren't you, Olivier?"

He grunted *yes,* then returned to the Game Boy he was fiddling with.

Never again did he come to our house or even call me by name. I hadn't realized until then how terribly flattered I'd been by his attention the previous year, by the idea that no matter where I was or what I was doing, someone was thinking of me, perhaps even longing for me. Is this how a teacher feels after a student's crush has faded?

The more French I learned, the more I understood how fractured the Gs' relationship was with their daughter, Olivier's mother, who eventually broke off contact with her parents and prevented them from seeing their grandsons. Clotilde died, and Madame G's mother followed not long afterward, at the age of 103. I saw Olivier a few years later, just before Hugh and I packed up and moved to Sussex. He was working in his hometown, at the hypermarket his grandparents used to take me to. I'd say he was around twenty at the time, dressed in jeans and a polo shirt. Over this he wore a synthetic red uniform jacket with short sleeves. I watched from a distance as he removed the security tag from a pair of slacks. Then he folded them, scanned a few grocery items, and frowned vacantly into space as the customer opened her purse and began searching for her credit card. Under the harsh lighting that casts no shadows, his skin was sallow. He looked empty.

Is this all? I wondered, feeling almost angry. *No going to university, no moving to a big, exciting city to become the next Mugler or Gaultier? Just working as a cashier at Intermarché, of all places?* Of course, I wasn't doing much when I was his age. It was, in fact, one of the worst years of my life. I was a college dropout, living in my parents' basement and getting high all day. Hopefully Olivier was just stalled, lingering at the gate a moment before taking off. Still, I thought as I headed out the door to where I'd parked my bike, I'd wanted so much more for this boy: not just Paris, but the world.

A Speech to the Graduates

Thank you so much for having me, and for presenting me with this honorary degree. It's not necessarily better than the one I earned by going to classes and putting myself into debt, but I'm trying to collect a stack of them before I die, so I really appreciate it. And congratulations, graduates. This is quite an accomplishment.

Like most of you, I am incredibly grateful for the education I received. A good public school followed by college. I went to three in all, looking for the right fit. The first two were OK, I guess, but midway through my sophomore year I got heavily into drugs and dropped out. Everyone said that was it—I'd made an irreparable mistake at age twenty and could never correct it. But I did. The place that I eventually graduated from, the School of the Art Institute of Chicago, has its qualities but is nowhere near Oberlin when it comes to academics. It might be different now, but in 1984, if you could draw Snoopy on a cocktail napkin, you were in. I received my bachelor of arts degree in 1987, when I was thirty.

Our commencement speaker was a conceptual artist named Vito Acconci. He'd done a lot but was best known for constructing a wooden ramp in a New York gallery. Then he hid beneath it and masturbated for several weeks without stopping.

"Well, *you* could do that!" my mother said when I explained to her who he was. "I mean, isn't that the goal? Doing what you love *and* getting paid for it!"

I don't think she understood a word of the man's commencement address. I'm not sure I did either. In preparing for today, I asked myself what he might have said that would have had an effect on my future.

I figured my post-college life would be pretty much like the one I'd been leading for the past decade: work some little job I didn't have to put much thought into, then come home and do my own stuff. It was the life that most of my friends led, and half my family.

My sister Gretchen went to RISD for painting. Then there was Amy at Second City. And, boy, did our father give us grief about it. "Art or comedy is all well and good, but you need to find something to fall back on," he'd say.

I hear this from parents all the time when I meet them at book signings. "Our daughter is an aspiring writer, and we told her that's fine, but she needs to find something to fall back on."

"So she's a terrible writer?" I ask.

"Well, no."

"Is she lazy? Has she shown no improvement since she started?"

"Of course not," the parents say. "She's wonderful. Writing is all she cares about."

"Then why does she need to fall back?" I ask. "Are you saying you have no faith in her before she's even had a chance to prove herself?"

It's an unfair question on my part, as it makes the parents sound unsupportive. What they mean is that they don't want their child to be broke and to suffer rejection. But there are plenty of worse things. At twenty-two, you are *built* for poverty and rejection. And you know why? Because you're good-looking. You might not realize it this morning, but thirty years from now, you will pull out pictures of yourself taken on this day and think, *Why did nobody tell me I was so fucking attractive?* You maybe can't see it now because you're comparing yourself to the person next to you, or two rows up. But you are stunning.

And let me tell you something else: when you're on your deathbed, or at least, say, sixty-one, the time you'll look back on most fondly will not be the day you bought your first Picasso painting at Sotheby's, the little still life done in 1921—oh, am I alone in this?—but the years after you graduated, when you were first living as an adult and everything seemed so possible. Maybe nothing worked out the way you planned, but you still thought it would, were convinced that it would. You were most likely broke and living in some crummy apartment. But it was *your* apartment, and you were good-looking. I guess I'm saying that these next few years could be the best of your lives. Just don't blow it.

But how? you're thinking. I was going to tell you not to rush into anything. "Don't become an adult quite yet. Take a wild chance, and whatever you do, *don't* move back to your hometown. *Especially* don't move back in with your parents."

But who am I to say that to a twenty-two-year-old owing $120,000? I'm not sure your generation has the luxury of drifting across the globe, trying this for a while and then that. How do you find yourself when, before you've even started, you find yourself in debt?

So there goes that advice.

Here, though, are a few things I *can* tell you:

One. When it comes to scented candles, you really need to watch it. There are basically only two brands worth having: Trudon and Diptyque. *I can't afford that!* you're probably thinking. *Not with this $120,000 debt for my degree in dance history.* To this I say, "Fine. You'll just have to go *without* scented candles until you can afford Diptyque or Trudon, or until someone gives them to you."

Two. Choose one thing to be terribly, terribly offended by—this as opposed to the dozens or possibly hundreds that many of you are currently juggling.

Three. Stand up for what you believe in, as long as I believe in the same thing. Those of you who'd like to ban assault rifles, I am behind you 100 percent. Take to the front lines, give it your all, and don't back down until you win. Do not, however, petition to have a Balthus painting removed from the Met because you can see the subject's underpants. The goal is to have *less* in common with the Taliban, not more.

Four. Be yourself. Unless yourself is an asshole. *How will I know if I'm an asshole?* you're probably wondering. Well, pay attention. Do people avoid you? Every time you park the car or do your laundry, do you wind up engaged in some sort of conflict?

An example: Not to pat myself on the back, but I've been doing some work the past few years with a group called Love Hope Strength. What they do is get people to donate bone marrow, and what I like is that they allow me to tell outrageous lies about them. "If you sign up," I promise audiences at my readings, "you will get to have sex with the most attractive member of the cancer patient's family—young or old, they cannot by law refuse you."

People don't donate their bone marrow *in* the theater, of course. Rather, someone swabs the inside of their cheek, and they fill out a quick form. It's rare to find a match, but it does happen. The cutoff age is fifty, so I tell the audience that. Then I announce that whoever registers with Love Hope Strength can come right to the front of the book-signing line. This is how you get your donors. That said, if I have, say, two thousand people in the theater, fifty might take the bait. That doesn't sound like much, but it's actually a good number, and if you're going to forty cities, it adds up.

So I'm in Napa, California, and this woman, maybe around sixty-five, claims that I'm being ageist, and that if I don't let her cut to the front of the book-signing line, she's going to take the producer of the show to court and sue for discrimination. Now, this is a fairly small theater. I have twenty people who've signed up to donate bone marrow. I'd told the audience it doesn't hurt at all, that they can, in fact, undergo the extraction *while* they're having sex with the cancer patient's family member of their choice. This is the biggest lie of all, as it is, in truth, an excruciating procedure. Here are twenty people willing to endure a great deal of discomfort, not to benefit someone they know but to possibly save the life of a complete stranger. That, to me, is real heroism. And this woman says that unless I let her come to the front of the line, she'll sue. She's taking her selfish desire to get home as quickly as possible and masking it as a fight against injustice.

Now *that's* an asshole, the person you never want to be. I wrote in her book, "You are a horrible human being." And of course she laughed, thinking I was kidding. That's the drawback to writing humor. People always think you're kidding. "No, I mean it," I told her. "You're awful."

She laughed harder.

Five. Always have a few jokes up your sleeve. They come in handy at casual get-togethers and probably don't hurt at job interviews either, depending on what position you're applying for. Here's one my friend Ronnie told me that's timely, quick, and easy to remember:

It's night, and a cop stops a car a couple of priests are riding in. "I'm looking for two child molesters," he tells them.

The priests think for a moment. "We'll do it!" they say.

Six. This last bit of advice is one very few of you are going to take, which is unfortunate, as it's just as important as what I told you about scented candles. And it's this: write thank-you letters. On a practical level it's just common sense. People like doing things for people who are grateful. Say your grandmother gives you $100 as a graduation gift. If she has eight grandkids who are or will be in the position that you're in now, I guarantee that yours will be the only thank-you note—not an email or text or Facebook message, but an actual letter with a stamp on it—that she receives. And she will treasure it. Then, a few months down the line, you can write again, telling her that you just spent the last of the money she sent. "I was at Goodwill, buying a dress I can wear for my job interview tomorrow," you could say. "The skid marks will hopefully come out after the first wash, and as for the underarm stains, I guess we'll see. But as I was paying for it, I thought of how kind you've always been to me, and of how lucky I am to have you in my life."

Chances are around 80 percent that she'll send you more money. Not because you asked for it but because you're grateful. I've talked to employers who say that the applicants who send a thank-you letter after an interview go right to the top of the pile. When I go on a book tour, I write to everyone who interviews me, to every store and media escort. You know who else does that? Nobody.

It's not because they're not grateful—they *are,* most likely. Rather, they just think, *Oh, people will understand.* And they will, of course. Your grandmother's gotten used to sending you gifts and never hearing anything back. *Well,* she thinks, as you lie around, texting someone in the next room about something you've just seen on TV, *he's busy.*

But here's the thing: she's busy too, yet she takes the time to send you stuff. I'm not trying to be a guilt-monger. I'm trying to help you. And who am I? A fairly successful person, one with a Picasso painting and a number of books under his belt, who will go home at the end of this day and write to the president of Oberlin to thank her for this degree that I do not deserve but am so incredibly grateful for.

Hurricane Season

Grow up in North Carolina and it's hard to get too attached to a beach house, knowing, as you do, that it's on borrowed time. If the hurricane doesn't come this autumn, it'll likely come the next. The one that claimed our place in September 2018 was Florence. Hugh was devastated, while my only thought was *What's with the old-fashioned names?* Irma, Agnes, Bertha, Floyd—they sound like finalists in a pinochle tournament. Isn't it time for Hurricanes Madison and Skylar? Where's Latrice, or Category 4 Fredonté?

Florence, it was said, gave new meaning to the word *namaste* along the North Carolina coast.

"Are you going to evacuate?"

"Namaste."

Hugh and I were in London when the hurricane hit and was followed almost immediately by a tornado. Our friend

Bermey owns a house—the Dark Side of the Dune—not far from ours, and went over to check on the Sea Section as soon as people were allowed back onto the island. He found our doors wide open—blown open by the wind. A large section of the roof had been ripped off, and the rain that had fallen in the subsequent days had caused the ceilings on both floors to cave in, the water draining, as if the house were a sieve, down into the carport. Bermey took pictures, which looked so tawdry I was embarrassed to share them. It seems that rats had been living in the second-floor ceilings. So there were our beds, speckled with currant-sized turds and tufts of bloated, discolored insulation.

All the interior drywall would need to be replaced, as would the roof, of course, along with the doors and windows. We were left with a shell, essentially. Had ours been the only place affected, it might have been easy to have the repairs done, but between the hurricane and the flooding, thousands of homes had been either destroyed or severely damaged—and that was just in North Carolina.

Our other house, luckily, was relatively unscathed. It's next door to the Sea Section, and when it came up for sale in 2016, Hugh disregarded my objections and bought it. His argument was that if he didn't get it, someone would most likely tear it down and construct the sort of McMansion that has become the rule on Emerald Isle rather than the exception. The size of these new houses was one thing—eight bedrooms was common, spread over three or four stories—but what came with them, and what you *really* didn't want next door to you, was a swimming pool. "It happened to us ten years ago," moaned my friend Lynette, who owns an older, traditionally sized cottage up the street from us. "Now all we hear is 'Marco!' 'Polo!' over and over. It's like torture."

The place that Hugh bought is ancient by Emerald Isle standards—built in 1972. It's a single-story four-bedroom, perched on stilts and painted a shade of pink that's almost carnal. Like the Sea Section, it's right on the ocean, but unlike the Sea Section, it's rented out to vacationers. At first Hugh went through an agency, but now he does it himself through a number of websites. Our friend Lee across the street rents out his place, Almost Paradise, as do most of our Emerald Isle neighbors, and all of them have stories to tell: People leave with the pillows and coat hangers. People grill on the wooden decks. They bring dogs regardless of whether you allow them, and small children, meaning that all sorts of things get flushed down the toilets: seashells, doll clothes, dice. And, of course, people complain about absolutely everything: The TV gets only ninety channels! There's some missing paint on the picnic table!

Lee once got a comment from a renter that read, "I was shocked by your outdoor shower."

"I was thinking, *How surprising can it be?*" he told me. "I mean, you're at the beach, for God's sake. Then I went out to wash up, and when I touched the handle for the hot water, I got thrown clear across the room."

Hugh bought the second house with everything in it, and although it's a bit heavy on the white wicker, the furniture is far from awful. He drew the line at the artwork, though. It was standard fare for a beach house: garish pictures of sailboats and sunsets, signs reading, IF YOU'RE NOT BAREFOOT, YOU'RE OVERDRESSED and OLD FISHERMEN NEVER DIE, THEY JUST SMELL THAT WAY.

If he wanted to, Hugh could work as a professional forger—that's how good he is at copying paintings. So for the rental house he reproduced a number of Picassos, including *La Baignade* from 1937, which depicts two naked women knee-deep in the water with a third person looking on. The figures are abstracted, almost machinelike, and cement-colored, positioned against a sapphire sea and an equally intense sky. Hugh did three others—all beach-related—and got a comment from a renter, saying that while the house was comfortable enough the "artwork" (she put it in quotes) was definitely *not* family-friendly. As the mother of young children, she had taken the paintings down during her stay and said that if the owner wanted her to return, he'd definitely have to rethink his decor. As if they were *Hustler* centerfolds!

"Can you believe that woman?" Hugh said, almost a year after the hurricane hit, when we arrived to spend a week on Emerald Isle. It was August. The Sea Section was still under construction, so we stayed at the pink house, which he was calling the Pink House, for reasons I could not for the life of me understand. "It's just such a boring name," I argued.

"It really is," my sister Gretchen agreed. She'd pulled up an hour before we had and was dressed in a fudge-colored tankini. Her long hair is going silver, and was gathered in a burger-sized bun, not quite on the back of her head but not on top either. She had turned sixty earlier that week and looked as if she were made of well-burnished leather—the effect of age and aggressive, year-round tanning. The skin between her throat and her chest had gone crepey, and it bothered me to notice it. I cannot bear watching my sisters get old. It just seems cruel. They were all such beauties.

"Calling this the Pink House is just...nothing," she said.

Considering that the rental was next door to the Sea Section, the best name, in my opinion, was either the Amniotic Shack or Canker Shores. Both had been suggested by a third party and were far better than what I'd come up with.

"And what was that?" Gretchen asked, opening a cabinet in search of a coffee cup.

"Country Pride Strong Family Peppermill," I told her.

"Not that again," Hugh said.

"It's not a pun, but I think it has a nice ring to it."

Hugh opened the refrigerator, then reached for the trash can. Renters aren't supposed to leave things behind, but they do, and none of their condiments were meeting with his approval. "It sounds like you just went to the grocery store and wrote down words."

"That's exactly what I did," I told him.

"Well, too bad. It's *my* house and I'll call it what I want to."

"But—"

He tossed a bottle of orange salad dressing into the garbage. "But nothing. Butt out."

C-R-A-B, Gretchen mouthed.

I nodded in agreement and made pinching motions with my hands. It can sometimes be tricky having Hugh around my family. "What is his *problem?*" each of my siblings has asked me at one time or another, usually flopping down on my bed during a visit.

"What is *whose* problem?" I always say, but it's just a formality. I know who they're talking about. I've heard Hugh yell at everyone, even my father. "Get out of my kitchen" is pretty common, as is "Use a plate" and "Did I say you could start eating?"

I'd like to be loyal when they complain about him. I'd like to say, "I'm sorry, but that's my boyfriend of almost thirty years you're talking about." But I've always felt that my first loyalty is to my family, and so I whisper, "Isn't it horrible?"

"How can you stand it?" they ask.

"I don't know!" I say. Though, of course, I do. I love Hugh. Not the moody Hugh who slams doors and shouts at people—that one I merely tolerate—but he's not like that all the time. Just enough to have earned him a reputation.

"Why did you yell at Lisa?" I asked, the year that three of my sisters joined us for Christmas at our home in West Sussex.

"Because she came to the dinner table with a coat on."

"So?"

"It made her look like she wasn't staying," he said. "Like she was going to leave as soon as her ride pulled up."

"And...?" I said, though I knew exactly what he was saying. It was Christmas dinner, and it's a slippery slope.

One year you wear a down coat at the table, and the next you're dressed in a sweat suit eating cold spaghetti out of a pan in front of the TV. My sisters can say what they will about Hugh's moodiness, but no one can accuse him of letting himself go, or even of taking shortcuts, especially during the holidays, when it's homemade everything, from the eggnog to the piglet with an apple in its mouth. There's a tree, there are his German great-grandmother's cookies, he will spend four days in an apron listening to the "Messiah," and that's the way it is, goddammit.

Similarly, he makes the beach feel the way it's supposed to. A few years back, he designed a spiral-shaped outdoor shower at the Sea Section that we found ourselves using even in the winter. He grills seafood every night and serves lunch on the deck overlooking the ocean. He makes us ice cream with fruit sold at an outdoor stand by the people who grew it, and mixes drinks at cocktail hour. It's just that he's, well, Hugh.

When I get mad at someone, it's usually a reaction to something he or she said or did. Hugh's anger is more like the weather: something you open your door and step out into. There is no dressing for it, and neither is there any method for predicting it. A few months after we met, for example, he and I ran into an old friend of mine at a play. This was in New York in 1991. We thought we'd all go out to eat, then Hugh offered to cook at his apartment. Somewhere between the theater and Canal Street, his mood darkened. There was no reason. It was like the wind shifting direction. The making of dinner involved a lot of muttering, and when my friend sat down to eat, his chair gave way, causing him to tumble onto the floor.

I apologized, saying that the chair was already broken, and Hugh contradicted me: "No, it wasn't."

"Why would you say that?" I asked after my friend had hobbled home.

"Because it wasn't broken," he said.

"It doesn't matter," I explained. "The point was to make him feel less embarrassed."

"Too bad," Hugh said. "I can't hide who I am."

"Well, it's really important to try," I told him. "I mean, like, really, *really* important."

"Let me ask you two a question," Hugh said to Gretchen and me on our first afternoon at the Pink House that August. He opened the sliding glass door to the deck and invited us to sit on the rocking chairs out there. The nails that held them together had been weeping rust onto the unpainted wood for so long that I put a towel down so as not to stain my white shorts, and got snapped at for it.

"*Now,* please."

I took a seat. "Ready."

"OK, do you think those are rickety? That's what the renter who hated the paintings called them."

I settled in and swayed as much going side to side as I did back and forth. "Yes," I said. "*Rickety* is probably the best word for this, possibly followed by *kindling.*"

"This one too," Gretchen said.

"Well, you're just spoiled," Hugh told us. "There's nothing at all wrong with those rocking chairs." He stormed back into the house, and I heard the click that meant he had locked us out.

"Goddammit," Gretchen said. "My cigarettes are in there."

Lisa, Paul, and Amy couldn't make it to the beach this time. It was sad being on the island without them, but at least it left fewer people for Hugh to crab at. "If you want to raise your voice to someone, you might consider the contractors," I said in the living room the following morning, looking next door at our empty driveway and not hearing what I heard coming from other houses: the racket of hammers and Skilsaws.

"Why don't *you* call them?" Hugh asked. "I filled out all the insurance forms. I see to all the bills and taxes, so how about *you* take care of something for a change?"

I didn't respond but just sighed, knowing he wasn't serious. The last thing Hugh wants is me taking care of something. I wouldn't have paid him any mind, but Gretchen was in the room. I don't like seeing my relationship through her eyes. That said, I *do* like seeing my family from Hugh's vantage point. To him, we're like dolls cut from flypaper, each one of us connected to the other and dotted with foul little corpses.

"What is it with men adjusting their balls all the time?" Gretchen asked, staring down at her phone.

"Are you talking about someone specifically?" Hugh asked.

"The guys I work with," she said. "The landscaping crews. They can't keep their hands away from their crotches."

"It could be due to heat rash," I suggested, adding that touching your balls in public is now illegal in Italy. "Men did it to ward off bad luck, apparently."

"Hmmm," Gretchen said, turning back to her phone. "I was in a meeting a few weeks back, and when I took one of my shoes off, a roach ran out. It must have been hiding in there when I got dressed that morning."

"What does that have to do with anything?" Hugh asked.

I rolled my eyes. "Does it matter? It's always time for a good story."

"Your family," he said, like we were a bad thing.

That afternoon I watched him swim out into the ocean. Gretchen and I were on the beach together, and I remembered a young woman earlier in the summer who'd had a leg bitten off, as well as a few fingers. Squinting at the horizon as Hugh grew smaller and smaller, I said that if the sharks *did* get him I just hoped they'd spare his right arm. "That way he can still kind of cook and access our accounts online."

It's hard to imagine Gretchen's boyfriend crabbing at anyone. She and Marshall have been together almost as long as Hugh and I have, and I can't think of a gentler guy. The same can be said of Paul's wife, Kathy. My brother-in-law, Bob, might get crotchety every so often, but when he snaps at Lisa for, say, balancing a glass of grape juice on the arm of a white sofa, we usually think, *Well, she kind of deserved it.* Amy's been single since the midnineties, but I never heard her last boyfriend, a funny and handsome asthmatic, yell at anyone, even when he had good reason to.

Gretchen and I had been on the beach for all of twenty minutes before she did what she always does, eventually. "I went online recently and read all sorts of horrible comments about you," she said lazily, as if the shape of a passing cloud had reminded her of it.

I don't know where she gets the idea that I—that anyone—would want to hear things like this. "Gretchen, there's a reason I don't google myself. I really don't—"

"A lot of people just can't stand you."

"I know," I said. "It's a consequence of putting stuff out there—you're going to get reactions. That doesn't mean I have to regard them all."

Jeez, I thought, sprinting back to the house over the scorching sand and wondering which was worse—getting snapped at by Hugh or having to endure what Gretchen was doling out. While it's true that I don't read reviews or look myself up, I do answer my mail. A few months earlier, I'd been given 230 letters sent to me in care of my publishing house. I had responded to 180 already, and brought the remaining 50 to the beach, where I figured I'd see to 10 a day. Most were just what I'd always wanted: kind words from strangers. Every now and then, though, a complaint would come along. I'd like to say I brush them off, and I guess I do, in time. For days, though, and sometimes months, I'll be bothered. For example, a woman sent me her ticket stubs, plus her parking receipt, demanding that I reimburse her. She and her husband had attended a reading and apparently objected to my material. "I thought you were better than that," she scolded, which always confuses me. First off, better than what? I mean, a clean show is fine, but no finer than a filthy one. Me, I like a nice balance.

That aside, who *doesn't* want to hear about a man who shoved a coat hanger up his ass? How can you *not* find that fascinating? "What kind of a person *are* you?" I wanted to write back.

Sometimes after a hard day of answering angry letters or emails, after having an essay rejected or listening to Gretchen tell me how much a woman she works with thinks I suck, I'll go to Hugh and beg him to say something nice about me.

"Like what?" he'll ask.

"I shouldn't have to *tell* you. Think of something."

"I can't right now," he'll say. "I'm in the middle of making dinner"—as if I'd asked him to name all the world capitals in alphabetical order. I feel as though I'm always complimenting him. "You look so handsome tonight." "What a great meal you made." "You're so smart, so well-read," etc. It's effortless, really.

"I don't want to give you a fat head," he'll tell me, when I ask for something in return.

"My head is, like, the size of an onion. I'm begging you, please, enlarge it."

He says I get enough praise already. But it's not the same thing.

"OK," he'll say, finally. "You're persistent. How's that?"

*   *   *

I like coming to Emerald Isle in May. It's not too hot then, and most everyone in my family can take a week off. Ditto at Thanksgiving. August, though, is definitely something I do for Hugh, a sacrifice. The heat that month is brutal, and the humidity is so high, my glasses fog up. At home, in Sussex, I'd happily be walking twenty-two miles a day, but at Emerald Isle, at the height of summer, I'm lucky to get in fifteen, and even then I really have to force myself.

I don't like to aimlessly wander, especially in a place where thunderstorms can appear without warning. I need a destination, so I generally go to a coffee shop near the grocery store, usually with a couple of letters to answer. Back and forth I'll walk, making three or more trips a day. When Hugh and I lived in Normandy, he heard a local woman telling a friend about a mentally challenged man she often saw marching past her house. He wore headphones, she said, and looked at pictures while talking to himself.

That, of course, was me, but they weren't pictures I was holding. They were index cards with that day's ten new French vocabulary words on them.

In Sussex not long ago, an acquaintance approached me to share a similar story. Again I was identified as mentally challenged, this time because I was picking up trash and muttering to myself. Only I wasn't muttering—I was repeating phrases from my Learn to Speak Japanese or Swedish or Polish audio program. "The woman who saw you said, 'I just hope no one tries to take advantage of him,'" the acquaintance told me.

On Emerald Isle this August, it was German I was muttering.

I might have picked up an occasional bit of trash, but I wasn't carrying any equipment, just ziplock bags of hot dogs or thick-cut bologna to feed the snapping turtles in the canal.

We'd been at the beach for four days when I noticed a great many ant colonies in the dirt bordering the sidewalk between the strip mall the CVS is in and the one the grocery store is in. The ants were cinnamon-colored, hundreds of thousands of them, all racing about, searching for something to eat.

"Excuse me," I said that afternoon to the guy behind the counter at the hardware store. "I was wanting to feed some ants and wonder what you think they might like? How would they feel about bananas?"

The man's face and neck were deeply creased from age and the sun. "Bananas?" He took off his glasses and then put them back on. "Naw, I'd go with candy. Ants like that pretty good."

I bought a bag of gummy worms from beside the register, bit them into thirds, and, on my way back to the house, distributed them among the various colonies as evenly as I could. It made me happy to think of the workers presenting their famished queens with sugar and possibly being rewarded for it.

"You're out there feeding *ants candy*?" Hugh said that night at the table, when we were all discussing our day. "They don't need your help, and neither do the stupid turtles. You mess these things up by feeding them—you hurt them is what you do." It wasn't what he said that concerned me but rather his tone, which, again, I wouldn't have noticed if my sister wasn't there.

"Well, they seemed pretty happy to me," I said.

Gretchen patted my hand. "Don't listen to Hugh. He doesn't know shit about being an ant."

This was a relatively short beach trip. Renters were arriving on Saturday, so the three of us had to have the house clean and be out by ten a.m. Gretchen left a bit earlier than we did, and, though I was sorry to see her go, it was a relief to escape her judgment regarding the life I have built with Hugh. As it was, whenever anything good happened during that week, whenever he was cheerful or thoughtlessly kind, I wanted to say, "See, *this* is what my relationship is like—*this*!"

It was a three-hour drive to Raleigh. I had work to do, so while Hugh drove, I sat in the back seat. "Just for a little while," I said. I must have fallen asleep, though. After waking, I read for a bit, and the next thing I knew the car wasn't moving. "What's going on?" I asked, too lazy to sit up and look out the window.

"I don't know," Hugh said. "An accident, maybe."

I righted myself and was just attempting to hop into the front seat when Hugh advanced and tapped the car in front of us. "Now see what you made me do!"

"Me?"

I don't know anything about cars, but the one he'd hit was bigger than ours, and white. The driver was husky and pissed-off-looking, with the sort of large, watery eyes I'd expect to find behind glasses. "Did you just hit me?" he asked, walking toward us. He bent to examine his bumper, which seemed to be made of plastic and had a pale mark on it, possibly put there by us.

Hugh rolled down his window. "I maybe did, but just a little."

The man glared at what he probably assumed was an Uber driver making extra money by taking people to the airport, or wherever that gap-toothed dope in the back seat was headed. He gave his bumper another once-over, then the traffic started moving. Someone honked, and the man got back into his car. "Hit him again," I said to Hugh. "But harder this time. We need to show him who's boss."

"Will you please shut up?" he said. "As a favor to me. Please."

When we first got news that Hurricane Florence had all but destroyed the Sea Section, I felt nothing. Part of my indifference was that I had expected this to happen. It was inevitable. Then too I wasn't as attached to the place as Hugh was. I wasn't the one who'd be contacting the insurance company. I wouldn't be dropping everything to fly to North Carolina. It wouldn't be me picking turds off our beds or finding a contractor. In that sense, I could afford to feel nothing. After looking at the pictures Bermey had sent, I shrugged and went for a walk. At dusk, I returned and found Hugh in our bedroom, curled up with his face in his hands. "My house," he sobbed, his shoulders quaking.

"Well, *one* of your houses," I said, thinking of Florence's other victims. Some, like Hugh, were crying on their beds, far from the affected area, while others were on foldout sofas, in sleeping bags, in the back seats of cars, or on cots laid out like circuitry in public-school gymnasiums. People who'd thought they were far enough inland to be safe, who'd had real belongings in their now-ruined houses: things that were dear to them and irreplaceable. The hardest-hit victims lost actual people—mates or friends or family members swept away and swallowed by floodwaters.

Then again, this was something of a pattern for Hugh. So many of the houses he'd lived in growing up had been destroyed: in Beirut, in Mogadishu, in Kinshasa. He's actually sort of bad luck that way.

I put my arms around him and said the things that were expected of me: "We'll rebuild, and it will all be fine. Better, actually. You'll see." This was how I always imagined myself in a relationship: the provider, the rock, the reassuring voice of wisdom. I had to catch myself from saying, "I've got you," which is what people say on TV now when they're holding a distraught person. It's a nice sentiment, but culturally speaking, there was only a five-minute period when you could say this without sounding lame, and it has long passed.

I *do* have him, though. Through other people's eyes, the two of us might not make sense, but that works in reverse as well. I have a number of friends who are in long-term relationships I can't begin to figure out. But what do I know? What does Gretchen or Lisa or Amy? They see me getting scolded from time to time, getting locked out of my own house, but where are they in the darkening rooms when a close friend dies or rebels storm the embassy? When the wind picks up and the floodwaters rise? When you realize you'd give anything to make that other person stop hurting, if only so he can tear your head off again? And you can forgive and forget again. On and on, hopefully. Then on and on and on.

Highfalutin

When we were young, my sister Amy and I used to pretend that we had a hospitality show. I don't remember if we were supposed to be husband and wife or if we were just friends. Lex and Germalina, we called ourselves. I wish they'd been better names, but we were only twelve and eight at the time. "Today we're going to make fried chicken," Amy would say in an artificially bright voice. "And if your family is anything like mine, they're guaranteed to *llllove* it."

"And how!" I might add, or "Who doesn't like chicken?" She was at ease in front of the nonexistent cameras, while I tended to freeze up, qualities that would continue into our adulthood when the cameras became real. I go on talk shows and look like a hostage, my hands twisted in my lap, my eyes darting this way and that, counting the seconds until the host releases me. Amy, on the other hand, appears completely at home. People who watched her on *Letterman,* or see her now on *The Late Show* or *Later Than Late* or *Now It's So Late It's Actually Early,* think of her as bubbly. The word *quirky* gets tossed around as well, but she's neither of those things. In real life, Amy is thoughtful and low-key, more apt to ask a question than answer one.

Back in our Raleigh kitchen, I'd admire the way she could fake-smile and convincingly act as if something was burning. When it came to pretend, I was spent after twenty minutes, while she could go on all afternoon and well into the evening. "And how about some biscuits to go with that chicken?" she'd ask, positioning a number of rolled-up white socks on a baking sheet and popping them into the oven. "Mmmmm, buttery biscuits are what makes a house a home!"

Cut to fifty years later, when my sister actually had such a show. It wasn't as earnest as our childhood version, but its bones were the same, and it was nominated three times for an Emmy Award. *At Home with Amy Sedaris,* it was called, and its second season had just begun airing when Hugh and I—who'd left New York in 1998—returned, at least part-time, and got a place on the Upper East Side. A few days after moving in, I had to leave on a forty-five-city lecture tour, and by the time I got back, Hugh had essentially sprayed the place, the way a tomcat would, and made it his own.

"I actually caught him telling someone they had to come and see *his* new apartment," I said to Amy on the phone one afternoon. "*His!*"

She was dealing with a new place as well, though hers was downtown and in the same building she'd occupied for the past ten years. It's a one-bedroom in the West Village, and when its twin became available directly upstairs from her, she bought it. "I didn't want anybody loud to move in," she explained. Everyone assumed she'd build a staircase and join the two places, but she doesn't care to, in part because of her rabbit, a male named Tina who runs freely throughout her home, eating it. I learned years ago never to leave anything on a chair or, worse still, the floor. "I could have sworn these shoes had laces," I'd say before I wised up. How many times did I come upon my earbuds, wireless before they made them wireless? The last night I spent at her place, I awoke to find her previous rabbit, Dusty, chewing my eyelashes, which were, like, still connected to my lids.

Tina has gnawed holes in Amy's sofa and has taken to the underside of her very expensive bed the way a beaver might. If a cat had caused that much damage, OK, but I don't see the emotional payoff with a rabbit. The only reason they're not classified as rodents is that they have four incisors in the upper jaw rather than two—a technicality if ever there was one.

Without a staircase connecting the floors, Amy will be able to have unfortified electrical cords in the new apartment. The first thing she did after getting the keys was coerce Hugh into painting it. Not that he complained. My sister is the kind of person you want to do things for. I can't even call it manipulation. She says she needs something, and all you want to do is provide it.

*　　*　　*

When we both lived in New York, back in the nineties, Amy and I went by the name of the Talent Family and put on a number of plays together. She's not a writer in the traditional sense. She doesn't arrange words on paper; rather, she throws out ideas she becomes bored with between the time you jot them down in your notebook and the time you type them up in the form of a script. "I know I said it would be funny if my character's mother comes to visit," she'd say at three in the morning, both of us stoned and reading over the scene I'd constructed. "But what if she came *on a horse?*"

So the mother would arrive on a horse. Then Amy would decide it shouldn't be the character's mother—it should be her stepmother alone on the rear seat of a tandem bicycle. We smoked pounds of marijuana. We put on seven plays, and I never missed a single performance. I couldn't, really, as without someone keeping watch, all hell would break loose. Then too I didn't want to miss anything. The writer Douglas Carter Beane hired my sister to act in one of his plays and was later heard to say, "What do you call it when Amy Sedaris recites one of your lines? A coincidence."

"What the hell was going on out there?" I'd ask after a performance, more astonished than angry, really. I can never get angry with her.

"Well, people laughed," Amy would say, referring to something she'd improvised.

"Yes, but when your character says something like that, it completely undermines…"

"Oh, come on. It was funny."

And, of course, it was. I've never seen audiences laugh the way they did at those plays. Movies and TV can't capture what's special about Amy. She's not an actress, exactly, or a comedian but more like someone who speaks in tongues. As opposed to myself, and just about everyone I've ever known, she lives completely in the moment. "What was that funny thing you said yesterday when we saw that old blind woman get mowed down by a skateboarder?" I'll ask.

And she'll have no memory of it. When Amy gets going, it's like she's possessed.

The best moments of my life were spent in the dressing room, laughing with the cast and crew before a show. Never did I wish that I was going onstage myself. It felt good enough to sit in the back row, occasionally hearing a word I had written and watching the audience discover my sister. You sometimes couldn't tell if she was a man or a woman, and so people would poke one another, whispering as she stormed into a scene, "Who *is* that person?"

There are few greater pleasures than feeling proud of someone, of worrying you might burst with it, especially if that someone is related to you and therefore part of your organization. I've always thought of my family that way, as a company. What's good for one of us is good for all of us. Our jobs are to advance the name Sedaris.

We might have continued with the plays, but then I got a lecture agent and started going onstage myself, in a way that I was comfortable with—just reading out loud. Amy created a TV show with her old friends from Second City, and we continued on parallel tracks, always supporting each other and calling for advice. "What would be a good fake name for a fish restaurant?" one of us would ask. "For a polluted river? For a perfume worn by a street prostitute?"

"What would be a good fake name for some medication?" Amy asked in late May 2019, when we got together for lunch in New York. She'd just started working on the third season of her TV show, and I was enjoying a week in my new apartment between the end of my lecture tour and the start of my paperback tour.

We like going out for Greek food, so we met at a place called Avra on East 60th Street. Amy wore a long gingham dress from Comme des Garçons that made her look like a hostess at the Cracker Barrel, and when she waved and called out my name—we never hug—I noticed that she had a couple of teeth missing on the upper right side of her mouth: her first premolar and its neighboring cuspid. The gap left by their absence was big enough to stick your thumb through. "The latest was pulled three days ago," she told me as we were led to our table. "But you can't really notice it, can you?"

"Ummm, *yeah,*" I said, thinking of how hickish we must

have looked. My teeth splayed like a donkey's, and hers simply AWOL.

Amy's problem, though, was just temporary. "They gave me a flipper, but I can't really eat with it," she explained, adding that the gap would be plugged with implants, which would be installed over the coming year. "The dentist stuck a needle as long as a pencil into the roof of my mouth, and though I couldn't see myself, I'm sure I made a face I've never made before."

"I'm eventually getting implants for my two front teeth," I told her, opening my menu, "but I'm thinking that instead of central incisors side by side I'd like one single supertooth. Wouldn't that be funny?"

Our waiter looked Greek but was from Macedonia. "Really?" we said. "When did you move here? Where do you live now? Is your mom still back in your hometown? Does she cry easily?"

We're often accused of being overly curious, but doesn't it beat the alternative? Our mother was the same way. "Oh, Sharon, what does it matter whether or not the guy likes working here?" our father would say. "He's a nobody. He's nothing, a grown man pulling corks out of wine bottles." Our father was always horrible in restaurants. The last time he was with us in New York, he slammed the empty bread basket on the table and thundered at a passing busboy, "*Bread!*" When the waiter asked if we were ready for the check, my father said, "Are you ready to bend over and take it?"

"Which didn't even make sense," I said to Amy later that night. "In the first place, *I* paid, not Dad. He didn't even pretend to reach for his wallet. But that aside, wouldn't it be the *customer* who bends over and takes it?"

He always treated people in the service industry with contempt, so we were always extra warm and engaging, trying to make up for it.

After we'd ordered, and I had suggested *Highfalutin* as a good name for fake medication ("The doctor wants me on fifty milligrams of Highfalutin, but I think he's just full of himself"), Amy told me about a story she'd just read in the paper. "It was about this guy in Russia, I think, who came across a bear that broke his spine, then dragged him back into its cave. I guess bears do that—save things to eat later. So this man was there for a month, drinking his own urine. When they found him, his eyes were swollen shut and he looked like a mummy. I'll send you the picture."

This prompted me to bring up a woman I'd read about who was discovered in the parking lot of a Walmart somewhere or other. "She was drunk and riding around in one of those mobility scooters, a Jazzy or a Rascal, drinking white wine out of a Pringles can."

"A Pringles can!" Amy said. "Why didn't we think of that?"

People assume that if you're on TV and in movies, everyone you hang out with is an actor. My sister, though, is more apt to spend time with the Korean woman who is her dry cleaner, or a Queens retiree named Helen Ann, who used to run one of those Mail Boxes Etc.–type places and taught her, among other things, that a dollar bill is exactly six inches long. "Good to know if you need to measure something in a pinch," she'd said.

"How's Adam?" I asked, referring to a fellow in his late thirties who was a cheerleader in college and will do backflips on command.

"Great," she said. "He came over last Saturday and we took mushrooms. Then I decided we should cut up my bedroom carpet."

"So you were on mushrooms with razor blades in your hands?"

She nodded and speared one of the meatballs I had ordered as an appetizer. "Adam didn't think it was such a great idea either, but it worked out fine. Boy, we had fun."

The only thing I miss about being sober is not getting high with Amy. "I wish someone would just slip me something," I said, claiming the last meatball. "That way, it wouldn't be my fault, and technically I wouldn't have to start counting days again from zero. That's called a freelapse, apparently. Can you believe there's a word for it?" One big difference between my sister and me is that she can have drugs in her house for months on end. Her appetite isn't bottomless the way mine was. It's the same with alcohol. I don't think I've ever seen her finish a drink. In that regard, at least within our family, she is unique.

*   *   *

Amy insisted on paying for lunch, and then, because it was right across the street and we can't go more than two hours without buying something, we went to Barneys. When the uptown branch first opened in 1993, we came with our younger sister Tiffany, who was visiting from Boston and loudly said of everything she touched, "Holy fuck, this is more than my rent!"

She was on ecstasy, as was I, but still. "Keep it down," Amy and I said. Tiffany read our embarrassment as pretension, but it wasn't that. Her comments just weren't funny enough to be overheard. Amy and I couldn't afford anything at Barneys either, but still we defended its right to exist. We had no idea back then how drastically things would change—not just our fortunes but the world in general.

The saddest development in New York since I left twenty years ago is the rise of e-commerce. People are ordering everything online, and it's killing stores. It's horrible, the number of empty shop fronts you pass now.

"They're like missing teeth," I said to Amy. "I mean...oops."

She scowled like a jack-o'-lantern at the passing traffic. "It's so unfair that things have to change because of lazy people."

In the not-too-distant future, who knows what we'll be left with? Maybe that's why we shop so much now: because we can. When Amy comes to see me in London, it's one store after another. I make a schedule, with breaks so we can return to the house and drop off our bags. One of our favorite places there is Dover Street Market, which sells both crazy Japanese clothing *and* taxidermy—the best of both worlds. I'd seen a kiwi there a few months earlier. "It was the size of a chicken," I said as we walked into Barneys, "mounted on a thin plank of wood with its head lowered just slightly and this beautiful, delicate beak about four inches long. I asked the price and learned it was the equivalent of ten thousand dollars. 'It's a hundred years old,' the salesman told me, which I guess makes sense, but still."

"That's when you should have snapped the beak off and asked, 'How much is it now?'" Amy said.

Ten years ago, Barneys would have been full of shoppers on a Thursday afternoon, but now it was dead.

"I like your look," a lonely salesman said to me on the second floor. "Are you an architect?"

"These aren't architect glasses, are they?" I asked Amy as we proceeded upstairs. "Architects wear, like, scaffolding on their faces. These aren't nearly dramatic enough."

She considered a floor-length Balenciaga dress she found beside the register in one of the women's departments. It was pink and looked like a long shirt you'd cut the sleeves off of, roughly, with scissors. "I'm just going to try it on *over* what I'm wearing," she said to the salesclerk, slipping it over her head.

He was slim and wore very small, very tight shorts.

Amy was eyeing herself in the mirror. "I don't *need* it really, but I don't know. It's sort of nice." She looked at the hefty price tag and was trying to justify the cost when the salesman said that actually the dress was on hold for somebody else.

"Really?" Amy said. I could practically see the spirit

entering her body. Taking over. "On hold for somebody else?" She yanked the dress back over her head, bunched it up, and threw it on the floor. Briefly she glared down—no longer herself, but a character—and, just as I thought she might step on it or pretend to spit on it, she balled her hands into fists and stomped off down the escalator, the monster with two teeth missing, the terror in the Cracker Barrel dress.

"That was just...that was a joke," I explained to the clerk. "She's a...comedy person."

With Barneys a bust, we headed downtown to Comme des Garçons in a cab driven by a man with an unfortunate case of rosacea. "What's your idea of perfect happiness?" Amy asked me as the taxi passed a horse-drawn carriage on Central Park South. "Mine is sitting in first class with an ice cream sundae while watching a documentary about Jim Jones. That's just the best."

I thought for a moment. "My idea of happiness is being on tour, in a great hotel, and having enough time to take a long bath before I have to head to the theater."

They know us at Comme des Garçons, so they let us use the bathroom, which is just off the sales floor. After it was unlocked by a staff member, I stepped in to pee and thought how odd it was that my idea of perfect happiness—and Amy's too—involved being alone. Actually, I realized, *this* was my idea of it. Being with her, the two of us laughing and shopping together.

I was going to tell her as much, but when I opened the door, there she was. "Oh, Jesus," she called, her right hand pinching her nose, her shoulders hunched as if she might throw up. "David Sedaris, what in heaven's name did you do in there? My God, the stench!"

Everyone looked our way as, for the second time that afternoon, though not unhappily, I died.

Unbuttoned

I was in Paris, waiting to undergo what promised to be a pretty disgusting medical procedure, when I got word that my father was dying. The hospital I was in had opened in 2000, but it seemed newer. From our vantage point in the second-floor radiology department, Hugh and I could see the cafés situated side by side in the modern, sun-filled concourse below. "It's like an airline terminal," he observed.

"Yes," I said. "Terminal Illness."

Under different circumstances I might have described the place as cheerful. It was the wrong word to use, though, when I'd just had a CT scan and, in a few hours' time, a doctor was scheduled to snake a multipurpose device up the hole in my penis. It was a sort of wire that took pictures, squirted water, and had little teeth. These would take bites out of my bladder, which would then be sent to a lab and biopsied. So *cheerful*? Not so much, at least for me.

I'd hoped to stick out in the radiology wing, to be too youthful or hale to fit in, but, looking around the waiting area, I saw that everyone was roughly my age and either was bald or had gray hair. If anybody belonged here, it was me.

The good news was that the urologist I met with later that afternoon was loaded with personality. This made him the opposite of one I'd seen earlier that month, in London, when I'd gone in with an unmistakable urinary tract infection. The pain was a giveaway, as was the blood that came out when I peed. UTIs are common in women but in men are usually a sign of something more serious. The London urologist was sullen and Scottish, the first to snake a multipurpose wire up my penis, but, sadly, not the last. The only time he came to life was when the camera started sending images to the monitor he was looking at. "Ah," he trilled. "There's your sphincter!"

I've always figured there was a reason my insides were on the inside: so I wouldn't have to look at them. Therefore I said something noncommittal, like "Great!," and went back to wishing I were dead, because it really hurts to have a wire shoved up that narrow and uninviting slit.

The urologist we'd come to see in Paris looked over the results of the scan I'd just undergone and announced that they revealed nothing out of the ordinary. He also studied the results of the tests I'd had in London, including one for my prostate. My eyes had been screwed shut while it took place, but I'm fairly certain it involved forcing a Golden Globe Award up my ass. I didn't cry or hit anyone, though. Thus it annoyed me to see what the English radiologist who'd performed the test had written in the comment section of his report: "Patient tolerated the transrectal probe poorly."

How dare he! I thought.

In the end, a quick prostate check and the CT scan were the worst I had to suffer that day in Paris. After taking everything into consideration, the French doctor, who was young and handsome, like someone who'd play a doctor on TV, decided it wasn't the right time to take little bites out of my bladder. "Better to give it another month," he said, adding that I shouldn't worry too much. "Were you younger, your urinary tract infection might not have been an issue, but at your age, it's always best to be on the safe side."

That evening, Hugh and I took the train back to London and bought next-day plane tickets for the United States. My father was by then in the intensive care unit, where doctors were draining great quantities of ale-colored fluid from his lungs. His heart was failing, and he wasn't expected to live much longer. "This could be it," my sister Lisa wrote me in an email.

The following morning, as we waited to board our flight, I learned that he'd been taken from intensive care and put in a regular hospital room.

By the time we arrived in Raleigh, my father was back at Springmoor, the assisted living center he'd been in for the past year. I walked into his room at five in the afternoon and was unnerved by how thin and frail he was. Asleep, he looked long dead, like something unearthed from a pharaoh's tomb. The head of his bed had been raised, so he was almost in a sitting position, his open mouth a dark, seemingly bottomless hole and his hands stretched out before him. The television was on, as always, but the sound was turned off.

"Are you looking for your sister?" an aide asked. She directed us down the hall, where a dozen people in wheelchairs sat watching *The Andy Griffith Show.* Just beyond them, in a grim, fluorescent-lit room, Lisa and Kathy were talking to a hospice nurse they had recently engaged. "What's Mr. Sedaris's age?" the young woman asked as Hugh and I took seats.

"He'll be ninety-six in a few weeks," Kathy said.

"Height?"

Lisa looked through her papers. "Five feet six."

Really? I thought. My father was never supertall, but I'd assumed he was at least five-nine. Had he honestly shrunk that much?

"Weight?"

More shuffling of papers.

"One twenty," Lisa answered.

"Well, now he's just showing off," I said.

The hospice nurse needed to record my father's blood pressure, so we went back to his room, where Kathy gently shook him awake. "Dad, were you napping?"

When he came to, my father focused on Hugh. The tubes that had been put down his throat in the hospital had left him hoarse. Speaking was a challenge, thus his "Hey!" was hard to make out.

"We just arrived from England," Hugh said.

My father responded enthusiastically, and I wondered why I couldn't go over and kiss him, or at least say hello. Unless you count his hitting me, we were never terribly physical with each other, and I wasn't sure I could begin at this late date.

"I figured you'd rally as soon as I spent a fortune on last-minute tickets," I said, knowing that if the situation were reversed he'd have stayed put, at least until a discount could be worked out. All he's ever cared about is money, so it had hurt me to learn, a few years earlier, that he'd cut me out of his will. Had he talked it over with me, had he said, for example, that I seemed comfortable enough, it might have been different. But I heard about it secondhand. He'd wanted me to find out after he died. It would be like a scene in a movie, the wealthy man's children crowded into the lawyer's office: "And to my son David, I leave nothing."

When I confronted him about the will, he said he'd consider leaving me a modest sum, but only if I promised that Hugh would touch none of the money.

Of course, I told him no.

"Actually, don't worry," I said of the plane tickets. "I'll just pay for them with part of my inheritance...oops."

"Awww, come on now," he moaned. His voice was weak and soft, no louder than rustling leaves.

"I'm going to roll him over and examine his backside for bedsores," the hospice nurse said. "So if any of y'all need to turn away..."

I was in the far corner of the room, beneath a painting my father had made in the late sixties of a monk with a mustache.

Beside me was the guitar I was given in the fifth grade. "What's this doing here?" I asked.

"Dad had it restrung a few months ago and said he was going to learn how to play," Lisa told me. She pointed to a keyboard wedged behind a plaster statue of a joyful girl with her arms spread wide. "The piano too."

"*Now?*" I asked. "He's had all this time but decided to wait until he was connected to tubes?"

After the hospice nurse had finished, my father's dinner was brought in, all of it pureed, like baby food. Even his water was mixed with a thickener that gave it the consistency of nectar.

"He has a bone that protrudes from the back of his neck and causes food to go down the wrong way," Lisa explained. "So he can't have anything solid or liquid."

As Kathy spooned the mush into my father's mouth, Hugh picked the can of thickener up off the dinner tray, read the ingredients, and announced that it was just cornstarch.

"So how was your flight?" Lisa asked us.

Time crawled. Amber-colored urine slowly collected in the bag attached to my father's catheter. The room was sweltering.

"Was that dinner OK, Dad?" Lisa asked.

He raised a thumb. "Excellent!"

How had she and Paul and Kathy managed to do this day after day? Conversation was pretty much out of the question, so they mainly offered observations in louder than normal voices: "She was nice," or "It looks like it might start raining again."

I was relieved when my father got drowsy and we could all leave and go to dinner. "Do you want me to turn your TV to Fox News?" Lisa asked as we put our coats on.

"Fox News," my father mumbled.

Lisa picked up the remote, but when she jabbed it in the direction of the television, nothing happened. "I can't figure out which channel that is, so why don't you watch *CSI: Miami* instead?"

Amy arrived from New York at ten the following morning, wearing a black-and-white polka-dot coat she'd bought on our last trip to Tokyo. Instead of taking her straight to Springmoor, Hugh and I drove her to my father's place, where we met up with Lisa and Gretchen. Our dad started hoarding in the late eighties: a broken ceiling fan here, an expired can of peaches there, until eventually the stuff overtook him and spread into the yard. I hadn't been inside the house since before he was moved to Springmoor, and though Lisa had worked hard at clearing it of junk, the overall effect was still jaw-dropping. His car, for instance, looked like the one in *The Silence of the Lambs* that the decapitated head was found in. You'd think it had been made by spiders out of dust and old pollen. It was right outside the front door and acted as an introduction to the horrors that awaited us.

"Whose turd is this on the floor next to the fireplace?" I called out, a few minutes after descending the filthy carpeted stairs into the basement.

Amy looked over my shoulder at it, as did Hugh, and

finally Lisa, who said, "It could be my dog's from a few months ago."

I leaned a bit closer. "Or it could be—"

Before I could finish, Hugh scooped it up with his bare hands and tossed it outside. "You people, my God." Then he went upstairs to help Gretchen make lunch.

Continuing through the house, I kept asking the same question: "Why would anyone choose to live this way?" It wasn't just the falling-down ceilings or the ragged spiderwebs draped like bunting over the doorways. It wasn't the tools and appliances he'd found on various curbs—the vacuum cleaners with frayed cords or the shorted-out hair dryers he'd promised himself he would fix—but the sense of hopelessness they conveyed when heaped into rooms that used to seem so normal, no different in size or design from those of our neighbors, but were now ruined. "Whoever buys this house will just have to throw a match on it and start over," Gretchen said.

What struck me most were my father's clothes. Hugh gets after me for having too many, but I've got nothing compared to my dad, who must own twenty-five suits and twice as many sport coats. Dozens of them were from Brooks Brothers, when there was just the one store in New York and the name meant something. Others were from long-gone college shops in Ithaca and Syracuse, the sort that sold smart jackets and white bucks. There were sweaters in every shade: the cardigans on hangers, their sleeves folded in a self-embrace to prevent them from stretching; the V-necks and turtlenecks folded in stacks, a few unprotected but most moth-proofed in plastic bags. There were polo shirts and dress shirts and casual shirts from every decade of postwar America. Some hung like rags—buttons missing, great tears in the backs, as if he'd worn them while running too slowly from bears. Others were still in their wrapping, likely bought two or three years ago. I could remember him wearing most of the older stuff—to the club, to work, to the parties he'd attend, always so handsome and stylish.

Though my mother's clothes had been disposed of—all those shoulder pads moldering in some landfill—my father's filled seven large closets, one of them a walk-in, and hung off the shower-curtain rods in all three bathrooms. They were crammed into dressers and piled on shelves. Hats and coats and scarves and gloves. Neckties and bow ties, too many to count, all owned by the man who, since his retirement, seemed to wear nothing but the same jeans and same T-shirt with holes in it he'd worn the day before, and the day before that; the man who'd always found an excuse to skimp on others but allowed himself only the best. There were clothes from his self-described fat period, from the time he slimmed down, and from the years since my mother died, when he'd been out-and-out skinny, none of them thrown away or donated to Goodwill, and all of them now reeking of mildew.

I nicked a vibrant red button-down shirt from the fifties, noticing later that it had a sizable hole in the back. Then I claimed the camel-colored, moth-eaten beret I'd bought him on a school trip to Madrid in 1975.

"It suits you," Hugh observed.

"It matches your skin and makes you look bald," Amy said.

We were all in the dining room, going through boxes with more boxes in them, when I glanced over at the window and saw a doe step out of the woods and approach some of the trash on the lawn near the carport, head lowered, as if she'd followed the scent of fifty-year-old house paint hardened in rusted-through cans. "Look," we whispered, afraid our voices from inside the house might frighten her off. "Isn't she beautiful!" We couldn't remember there being deer in the woods when we were young. Perhaps our dogs had scared them off.

"Oh," Lisa said, her voice as soft as our father's, "I hope she doesn't step on a rusty nail."

Gretchen served Greek food for lunch, and afterward we drove to Springmoor. It was a Saturday afternoon in late February, cold and raining. Our father was in his reclining chair covered with a blanket when we arrived, not asleep but not exactly awake either. It was this new state he occasionally drifted into: neither here nor there. After killing the overhead lights, we seated ourselves around his room and continued the conversation we'd been having in the car.

"I asked Marshall to write Dad's obituary, but he doesn't feel up to it," Gretchen said.

The rest of us glanced over at our father.

"He can't hear us," Gretchen said. She looked at me. "So will *you* write it?"

I've been writing about my father for ages, but when it comes to the details of his life, the year he graduated from college, etc., I'm worthless. Even his job remains a mystery to me. He was an engineer, and I like to joke that up until my late teens I thought he drove a train. "I don't really know all that much about him," I said, scooting my chair closer to his recliner. He looked twenty years older than he had on my last visit to Raleigh, six months earlier. One change was his nose. The skin covering it was stretched tight, revealing facets I'd never before noticed. His eyes were shaped differently, like the diamonds you'd find on playing cards, and his mouth looked empty, though it was in fact filled with his own teeth. He did this thing now, opening wide and stretching out his lips, as if pantomiming a scream. I kept thinking it was in preparation for speech, but then he'd say nothing.

I was trying to push the obituary off on Lisa when we heard him call for water. Hugh got a cup, filled it from the tap in the bathroom, and stirred in some cornstarch to thicken it. My father's oxygen tube had fallen out of his nose, so we summoned a nurse, who showed us how to reattach it. When she left, he half raised his hand, which was purpled with spots and resembled a claw.

"What's on your...mind?" he asked Amy, who had always been his favorite and was seated a few yards away. His voice couldn't carry for more than a foot or two, so Hugh repeated the question.

"What's on your mind?"

"You," Amy answered. "I'm just thinking of you and wanting you to feel better."

My father looked up at the ceiling and then at us. "Am I...real to you kids?" I had to lean in close to hear him,

especially the last half of his sentences. After three seconds
he'd run out of steam, and the rest was just breath. Plus the
oxygen machine was loud.

"Are you what?"

"Real." He gestured to his worn-out body and the bag on the
floor half filled with his urine. "I'm in this new... life now."

"It'll just take some getting used to," Hugh said.

My father made a sour face. "I'm a zombie."

I don't know why I insisted on contradicting him. "Not
really," I said. "Zombies can walk and eat solid food. You're
actually more like a vegetable."

"I know you," my father said to me. He looked over at Amy
and at the spot that Gretchen had occupied until she left. "I
know all you kids so well."

I wanted to say that he knew us superficially at best. It's how
he'd have responded had I said as much to him: "You don't
know me." Surely my sisters felt the way I did, but something—
most likely fatigue—kept them from mentioning it.

As my father struggled to speak, I noticed his fingernails,
which were long and dirty.

"If I just... dropped out of the sky like this... you'd think I
was a freak."

"No," I said. "*You'd* think you were a freak, or at least
a loser."

Amy nodded in agreement and I plowed ahead. "It's what
you've been calling your neighbors here, the ones parked in
the hall who can't walk or feed themselves. It's what you've
always called weak people."

"You're a hundred percent right," he said.

I didn't expect him to agree with me. "You're vain," I continued. "Always were. I was at the house this morning and couldn't believe all the clothes you own. Now you're this person, trapped in a chair, but you're still yourself to us. You're like...like you were a year ago, but drunk."

"That's a very astute...observation," my father said. "Still I'd like to...apologize."

"For being in this condition?" I asked.

He looked over at Amy, as if she had asked the question, and nodded.

Then he turned to me. "David," he said, as if he'd just realized who I was. "You've accomplished so many fantastic things in your life. You're, well...I want to tell you...you...you won."

A moment later he asked for more water, and drifted midsip into that neither-here-nor-there state. Paul arrived, and I went for a short walk, thinking, of course, about my father, and about the writer Russell Baker, who had died a few weeks earlier. He and I had had the same agent, a man named Don Congdon, who was in his midseventies when I met him in 1994 and used a lot of outdated slang. "The blower," for instance, was what he called the phone, as in, "Well, let me get off the blower. I've been gassing all morning."

"Russ Baker's mother was a tough old bird," Don told me one rainy afternoon in his office on Fifth Avenue. "A real gorgon to hear him tell it, always insisting that her son was a hack and would never amount to anything. So on her deathbed he goes to her, saying, 'Ma, look, I made it. I'm a successful writer for the *New York Times*. My last book won the Pulitzer.'

"She looked up at him, her expression blank, and said, 'Who are you?'"

I've been told since then that the story may not be true, but still it struck a nerve with me. Seek approval from the one person you desperately want it from, and you're guaranteed not to get it.

As for my dad, I couldn't tell if he meant "You won" as in "You won the game of life," or "You won over *me,* your father, who told you—assured you when you were small and then kept reassuring you—that you were worthless." Whichever way he intended those two faint words, I will take them and, in doing so, throw down this lance I've been hoisting for the past sixty years. For I am old myself now, and it is so very, very heavy.

I returned to the room as Kathy was making dinner reservations at a restaurant she'd heard good things about. The menu was updated Southern: fried oysters served with pork belly and collard greens—that kind of thing. The place was full when we arrived, and the diners were dressed up. I was wearing the red shirt I'd taken from my father's closet and had grown increasingly self-conscious about how strongly it stank of mildew.

"We all smell like Dad's house," Amy noted.

While eating we returned to the topic of his obituary, and

what would follow. A Greek Orthodox funeral is a relatively sober affair, sort of like a Mass. I'd asked if I could speak at my mom's, just so there'd be a personal touch. If I were to revisit what I read that morning in 1991, I'd no doubt cringe. That said, it was easy to celebrate my mother. Effortless. With my father, I'd have to take a different tone. "I remember the way he used to ram other cars at the grocery store when the drivers—who were always women—took the parking spots he wanted," I could say. "Oh, and the time he found seventeen-year-old Lisa using his shower and dragged her out naked."

How could I reconcile that perpetual human storm cloud with the man I had spent the afternoon with, the one who never mentioned, and has never mentioned, the possibility of dying, who has taken everything life has thrown at him and found a way to deal with it? Me, on the other hand, after a half dozen medical tests involving the two holes below my waist, before even learning whether or not I *had* cancer, I'd decided I was tired of battling it. "Just let me die in peace," I said to Hugh after the French urologist stuck his finger up my ass.

Meanwhile, here was my father, tended to by aides, afforded no privacy whatsoever, and determined to get used to it. *Where did that come from?* I wondered, looking at my fried chicken as it was set before me. *And how is it that none of his children, least of all me, inherited it?*

Of all us kids, Paul was the only one to fight the do-not-resuscitate order. He wanted all measures taken to keep our father alive. "You have to understand," he said over dinner, "Dad is my best friend." He didn't say it in a mawkish or dramatic way but matter-of-factly, the way you might identify your car in a parking lot: "It's that one there." The relationship between my brother and my father has always been a mystery to my sisters and me. Is it the thickness of their skin? The fact that they're both straight men? On the surface, it seems that all they do is yell at each other: "Shut up!" "Go to hell!" "Why don't you just suck my dick!" It is the vocabulary of conflict, but with none of the hurt feelings or dark intent. While the rest of us may mourn our father's passing, only Paul will truly grieve.

"Hey," he said, taking an uneaten waffle off his daughter's plate, "did I tell you I just repainted my basement?" He found a picture on his phone and showed me what looked like a Scandinavian preschool, each wall a bold primary color.

"Let me see," Amy said. I handed her the phone and she, in turn, passed it to Lisa. It then went by the spots where Tiffany and Gretchen would be if Tiffany hadn't killed herself and Gretchen hadn't fallen asleep at her boyfriend's house earlier that evening, and on to Kathy, then to my niece, Maddy, and back to Paul.

We were the last party to leave the restaurant, and were standing out front in a light rain, when Amy pointed at the small brick house across the street. "Look," she cried, "a naked lady!"

"Oh my God," we said, following her finger and lowering our voices the same way we'd done ten hours earlier with the doe on my father's lawn.

"Where?" Lisa whispered.

"Right there, through the window on the ground floor," Hugh told her. He and Amy would later remark that the woman, who was middle-aged and buxom and wore her hair in a style I associate with the nineteen forties, made them think of a Raymond Chandler novel.

"What's she doing?" I asked, watching as she moved into the kitchen.

"Getting a drink of water?" Lisa guessed.

Paul turned to his daughter. "Look away, Maddy!"

When the light went out, we worried that we had scared the naked woman, but a second later it came back on, and she was joined by a dark-haired man with a towel around his waist. The two of them appeared to speak for a moment. Then he took her by the hand and led her into another room and out of sight.

It was all we talked about as we made our way down the street to our various cars. "Can you believe it? Naked!" As if we'd seen a flying saucer, or a congregation of pixies. To hear us in a gang like that, the wonder in our voices, the delight and energy, you'd almost think we were children.

Themes and Variations

One of the things that most delighted me when I moved to Chicago in 1984 was the main branch of the public library, which was like a palace and was stocked with story collections I would've never found back home in Raleigh. Another pleasant surprise was my local bookstore, which was well within walking distance of my apartment and hosted author events. How thrilling it was to literally sit at the feet of writers I admired. I was too broke to afford hardcovers, so would usually get in line with a paperback, wondering as I waited, *What will I say?* Everything I thought of sounded inane, and by the time I got up to the signing table I was most often a stammering mess.

The kindest of these authors would notice my trembling hands and go out of their way to set me at ease. It wasn't that hard on their part, really—a quick question, a comment. "Do you live around here?" "Those shoes look like you made them yourself. Are you a cobbler?" Others would simply look up and nod as I blathered away. Then I'd thank them and flee, my face burning.

My worst experience still angers me all these years later. I waited in line, a nervous wreck, and when I got up there, the author was talking to someone—her publicist, maybe. "I don't know," she said, sounding bored. "There's not really much to do in this town. Why don't you call Jerry and see what he thinks?" My copy of her memoir was reached for, signed with nothing but her name, and then pushed back. She didn't even look up.

In that case I didn't leave embarrassed. I left feeling betrayed. What I'd wanted, much more than the book—which I would now rather die than read—was to be seen by this person. If only for a few seconds. I left the store determined that when and if it was ever *my* turn and *I* was the author seated at that table, I was going to engage people until they grew old, or at least thirsty. "Well, all right, then," they'd say, looking past me for the nearest exit, "let me let you go."

I would see them until they wilted.

And that's pretty much how it goes. I generally start the conversation immediately—that way the person wanting a book signed never has to say the things they'd stood in line agonizing over and will most likely regret later on. There are exceptions, though. I was in Baton Rouge in late May 2013 when a woman approached, saying, before I had a chance to throw her off-balance, "You got me to put my bra back on."

I set down my pen. "I beg your pardon?"

"I take it off the second I get home from work, and that usually means it's off for the night," she told me. "It means I'm not going anywhere for any reason. Then a friend called and told me you were here, so I put it back on and dashed over to see you!"

"Well...thank you," I said.

I repeated the woman's story the following evening in Atlanta, thinking it might get a nice response. It did, but the laughs were ones of recognition rather than surprise. "Do you take *your* bra off the moment you return from work?" I asked the first person in line. She was big-breasted, with short, pewter-colored hair, and she laid her book upon the table, saying, "Baby, I take it off *before* I get home."

"At the office?" I asked.

"No," she told me. "In the car."

"You take your blouse off?"

"Ain't no need to do that," she said. "What you do is unhook it in the back and then pull it out your sleeve."

"And after it's off, is it off for the night?"

"You know it is," she confided. "A friend will call drunk, wanting a ride, and I'll say, 'Honey, I got my bra off. Get yourself a cab.'"

Next in line was a male college student. "I can always tell when my mom borrows my car because she leaves her bra in the glove compartment."

I thought this was just an American phenomenon, but then I started my UK tour and learned that I was wrong. "Once this comes off, I'm in for the rest of the evening," women told me in London and Manchester and Liverpool. I did sixteen events. The last was in Edinburgh. "Do you remove your bra on your way home from work?" I asked a young woman with orange hair.

She nodded.

"In your car?"

"Oh no," she told me. "I do it on the bus."

All around me, this has been going on—for centuries—and I had no idea. Me, who grew up with a mother and four sisters!

It's not like the clues weren't there. How many times have I knocked on a woman's door after dark and had her answer wearing a sweatshirt that doesn't seem to go with the rest of her outfit, or with her arms crossed over her chest? I thought that was sign language for "Couldn't you have told me you were coming?" Now I see that it actually meant "If you think I'm putting my bra back on for this bullshit, you are so sorely mistaken."

When I'm lucky, while I'm out on tour a theme will develop. It can't be anything I force. Rather, it needs to be organic. For one book it was bras, and for the next it was jokes. It started with one a driver named Bill Mooney told me:

A Jewish fellow named Saul Epstein owns a nail company, very successful, and when he retires he hands it over to his son-in-law. Then he moves to Florida, and is there one day, reading the *New York Times,* when he comes upon a full-page ad. It's a picture of Jesus hanging on the cross, and below him are the words THEY USED EPSTEIN NAILS.

Furious, the old man reaches for the phone. "Are you out of your mind? That's no way to sell our product!"

The son-in-law promises to fix everything, and a week later, Epstein opens his *Times* to find another full-page ad. This one shows a cross standing empty on a hilltop. In front of it, lying with his face in the dust, is Jesus Christ, and on either side, looking down at him, are two Roman soldiers along with the words THEY DIDN'T USE EPSTEIN NAILS.

I repeated the joke at a bookstore that night and got the following:

What's the worst thing you can hear while you're blowing Willie Nelson?

"I'm not really Willie Nelson."

And: It's late at night and a man is getting ready to go to bed when he hears a knock on his door. He opens it and looks down to see a snail. "Yes," it says, "I'd like to talk to you about buying some magazine subscriptions."

Beside himself with rage, the man rears back, kicks the snail as hard as he can, and storms off to bed.

Two years later there comes another knock. The man answers and again he finds the snail, who looks up at him and says, "What the fuck was that all about?"

The following evening, at another bookstore, a man approached, saying, "So God tells Adam, 'I'm going to make you a wife, a helpmate, the most beautiful woman who ever lived. She'll be fantastic in bed, uncomplaining, and adventurous. The thing is, it'll cost you.'

" 'How much?' Adam asks.

" 'An eye, an elbow, a collarbone, and your left ball.'

"Adam thinks for a moment, then asks, 'What can I get for a rib?' "

This was countered an hour later with: Three friends marry three women from different parts of the world. The first chooses a Spanish girl and tells her on their wedding night that she has to do the dishes and the laundry, and to generally keep the house in order. It takes a while to break her in, but on the third day he comes home to find things as he wanted.

The second man marries a Thai girl. He gives his wife orders that she is to do all the cleaning as well as the cooking and ironing. The first day he doesn't see any results, but the following one is better. On the third day he finds that his house is clean, the dishes are done, and there's dinner on the table.

The third man marries an American girl. He orders her to keep the house clean, the dishes washed, and the lawn mowed, and to put hot meals on the table every evening. The first day he doesn't see anything. The second day he doesn't see anything either. But by the third day, some of the swelling has gone down. He can make out basic shapes with his left eye, and his arm has healed well enough that he can throw together a sandwich and load the dishwasher. He still has some difficulty when he urinates.

Not everyone was skilled with their delivery. "OK," someone might start, "a priest and a rabbi, or no...wait, a witch doctor and a priest and a rabbi go to a...oh gosh, just give me a second..."

By the end of the month I had close to two hundred jokes,

some not worth repeating, and others gold. I put them in a file on my computer and then categorized them, later noticing the significant overlap between *sex* and *misogynist*. Also, who knew there were so many pedophile jokes out there? Everyone seems to have one up their sleeve.

On my next book tour the theme was monkeys, and on the latest one it was items men shove inside themselves and later have to go to the emergency room to have extracted. This started when an ER nurse told me about a patient she'd seen earlier in the week who had pushed a dildo too far up his ass. The door had shut behind it, so he'd tried fishing it out with a coat hanger. When that proved the wrong tool for the job, he'd snipped it with wire cutters, then gone after both the dildo and the cut-off hanger with a sturdier, fresh hanger. You hear this from doctors and nurses all the time: their patients shove light bulbs inside themselves, shampoo bottles, pool balls...and they always concoct some incredible story to explain their predicament. "I tripped" is a big one.

And, OK, I'm pretty clumsy. I trip all the time, but never have I gotten back on my feet with a pepper grinder up my ass, not even a little bit. I'm pretty sure I could tumble down all the stairs in the Empire State Building—naked, with a greased-up rolling pin in each hand and a box of candles around my neck—and still end up in the lobby with an empty rectum.

Another common excuse is "I accidentally sat on it." Implied is that you were naked at the time and this can of air freshener that just happened to be coated with Vaseline went all the way up inside you. "I must have left it on the sofa when

I came home from work and took a shower. Then I sat down to watch the news the way I usually do, and, well, you know the rest."

A week into my tour—again because I'd mentioned the story onstage—a nurse handed me an X-ray of a man's pelvis with a set of hand weights in it. *How on earth?* I thought, imagining the work that must have taken. And to follow the first with a second? Who does that? Days later I saw an X-ray of a Bose speaker inside someone. "And it was still connected to Bluetooth," the woman who showed it to me whispered.

A parallel theme that June was money. On a book tour, you're generally accompanied by a media escort. This is a person who picks you up at the airport and takes you to all your interviews and appointments. In Milwaukee it was Mary. She's a handsome woman, maybe a few years older than I am, and we were heading to my hotel when she mentioned an event she had attended earlier in the day that was sponsored by her church. "There was a speaker, and at the end of his talk he gave everyone in the room a crisp new fifty-dollar bill and told us to go out into the world and pass it on to someone who needed it." She pushed her blond hair off her shoulder and checked her rearview mirror. "Oh, and it has to be done by 3:16. That corresponds to a Bible verse, though I don't remember which one."

Mary had a few hours between dropping me off at my hotel and returning at 5:00 to take me to the bookstore but explained that she wouldn't be around any poor people between now and then. "So, if it's not too much trouble, could *you* maybe pass the fifty on for me?"

I couldn't think of a better way to spend the afternoon. All I knew starting out was that I didn't want to give the money to a beggar. Better, I decided, to hand it to someone who was working a terrible job. So I went off in search of a McDonald's, figuring I'd hand the bill to the roughest-looking employee I could find. "Excuse me," I'd say. "Are you poor? Are you in debt?"

I hadn't brought my phone and didn't know where to find a McDonald's, so I just wandered. A half-dozen blocks from the hotel I came across a Subway, but I can't bear the smell of those places. I still had an hour before 3:16 but wanted as much time as possible in my comfortable hotel room before leaving for the bookstore. *OK,* I thought, looking at my watch, *I guess a beggar will do.*

But suddenly I didn't see any, which, I mean, isn't that always the way? When you just want to be left alone, they're everywhere and super-aggressive. Portland, Oregon's are the worst. They're all tattooed there and are stretched out on the sidewalk. Eighteen, twenty years old, with pierced noses and ears with so many holes in them you could likely tear off the outer rims the way you'd separate a stamp from a sheet. "Asshole," they spit as you walk by with your eyes averted. "Go fuck yourself."

I'd have welcomed a tough young Portland beggar in Milwaukee, but everyone I passed looked, if not well-off, then at least middle-class—all on cell phones, carrying shopping bags.

I saw an exhausted-looking man with a pillowcase standing on a corner but veered away when he raised a can of beer to his mouth.

No drinkers, I thought, sounding like a church lady.

By this point it was 2:58, and I was starting to panic, thinking, I guess, that if I didn't give the money away by 3:16, the God I claim not to believe in, the one whose only son was used to sell nails in one of my favorite jokes, was going to smite me.

It was then that I came upon the library—*Bingo,* I thought. That's poor-person central, at least in the United States, where such places double as homeless shelters. This was an old branch, and the building was grand. Inside, it was cool and tomblike. I saw two young women in their early twenties standing near the information desk, but everyone else was seated—slumped, for the most part—many with knapsacks and duffel bags on the floor beside them. None was convincingly reading. The books seemed more like props, something to stare into the way my father ended up staring at magazines, turned to the same page for hours on end.

I walked up to the counter. "How can I help you?" a librarian asked. She looked to me like a librarian is supposed to, slightly stern, with a longer-than-average neck.

"This might sound strange," I told her, "but I have fifty dollars to give to a poor person by 3:16. I see some pretty good candidates here and was wondering if you might direct me to the neediest of them."

The two young women standing nearby had apparently listened in.

"Give it to me," one of them said. She wore a lot of foundation and her eyebrows qualified as drawings. "I want fifty dollars." The T-shirt she had on was white and bedazzled with plastic gems. Because of the notebooks she and her friend were carrying, I guessed them to be community college students, possibly majoring in not giving a fuck.

Had a stranger approached me with a fifty-dollar bill when I was in college, I would have never forgotten it. In the mid-to-late eighties that was a lot of money, one-quarter of my rent, though I probably would have spent it on luxury items—pot, most likely, and some decent groceries, which at the time meant Marie's salad dressing. It came already refrigerated in a jar and was sold beside the lettuce at a store called Treasure Island. I'd have bought Green Goddess, or Creamy Ranch. Then I'd have gotten high and dipped things into my precious, precious dressings.

More than the pot and groceries, I'd have appreciated a short break from the constant stress I felt. Was there a single moment back then when I wasn't worried about money? When I wasn't concerned that a check might bounce or a higher-than-average phone bill would reduce me to eating pancakes for a week? I don't recall buying anything thoughtlessly. If chicken backs or boxes of spaghetti were ten cents cheaper five miles away, I would get on my bike in subzero weather and ride there. Meanwhile I'd see people as broke as, or broker than, I was at the expensive corner stores, buying milk and bread with their food stamps. They didn't know how to shop, hadn't been taught the way my sisters and I had, by a father who clipped coupons and bought all our produce from what amounted to a purgatory bin, the one things were emptied into just before they went to the dumpster. All our canned goods were dented and off-brand. Some had just one word on the label: BEANS, say, or CORN.

I could see how the girl at the counter might have needed the money. The problem was that she'd *asked* for it. "Asking doesn't cost a thing," people like to say, or, "If you don't ask, you don't get." But I think it's overrated—your reward for being pushy, though not for being interesting or particularly deserving. *Do I think this way because* I'm *unable to ask for things?* I wondered. *Have I spent the afternoon looking for the young, hapless version of myself, the person I was before my luck kicked in?*

"Give it to me," the young woman demanded, sounding more strident now.

"Let me put you in touch with our security guard," the librarian said. "She'll be able to help you much better than I can."

It was eight minutes after 3:00.

"I *need* fifty dollars," the college student repeated. "I want it."

Her friend chimed in then. "Me too. Give it to me."

At what point does this become robbery? I wondered.

The security guard was in her seventies and brittle. Her uniform had short sleeves and exposed her arms, which were twig-thin, like a snowman's. *This is who you call in case of trouble?* I thought. The woman had all the authority of a crumpled leaf.

"You're looking for someone poor?" She squinted through her oversized glasses at the far side of the room. "We got a lot of them today. But, oh, how about him?"

She gestured with her chin to a sorrowful-looking man in his sixties I had noticed earlier. What I'd honed in on, besides his duffel bag and the unconvincing way he was reading, was how shitty his haircut was. It looked like he'd done it himself with a campfire.

I walked over to him. "Excuse me."

He either couldn't hear me or was ignoring me.

"Sorry to bother you," I said a bit louder. "But would you please take this for me?"

I laid the fifty dollars on the table beside him.

"Sure," he said, as if he were doing me a favor.

The young woman at the counter narrowed her eyes. "Shit."

Her friend offered a slight variation. "Shithead."

Done, I thought. *And with six minutes to spare. Take that, God.*

"It was actually really smart of that speaker to hand out fifty-dollar bills," I said to Mary when she arrived to take me to the bookstore. The afternoon had left me high, almost, and words gushed from my mouth like water from a fire hose. "It made me think of all sorts of things: how good I have it, how I judge people, the arbitrary rules we set. Then too it makes for an interesting story. Give away fifty dollars of your own money, and the moment you tell someone about it you're an asshole. I mean, the one thing you're really *not* allowed to bring up in this world is your generosity. Because the moment you do, it's not generosity anymore—by bringing it to light, you've killed it. Plus, it makes the people you tell feel *un*generous, and they wind up hating you."

Mary nodded.

"And there's no point in me doing anything if I can't write about it," I continued. "It would be like...walking ten miles without my Fitbit on—a complete waste. I mean, I *do* do things I don't commit to paper: I use the bathroom, I have sex. But I try to be quick about it."

The following night in Duluth I mentioned the speaker that was still connected to Bluetooth, and a nurse told me about a guy who'd put his glass dildo in the freezer. When he later forced it up his ass, the extreme temperature change caused it to shatter, which led to all sorts of damage. After cringing, I thought of how someone—possibly me—should introduce the Chilldo, which would perhaps be made of Pyrex and thus guaranteed not to crack or fracture deep inside a user's rectum. I made a note to put it on my Million Dollar Idea list, just below a chain of airport barbershops called O'Hair. *Is this why I'm not poor?* I wondered. *Because I'm always thinking?*

I told the story about Mary that night as well, and at the end of the evening a woman handed me a fifty-dollar bill and asked that I give it away to someone who needed it.

I figured I'd wait until I reached St. Louis, but near my gate in Minneapolis, where I had a short layover the following afternoon, there was a McDonald's and, walking by it, I noticed a woman behind the counter. She was perhaps in her early fifties and significantly overweight, with dull gray hair that fell to her jawline. Her glasses were oval-shaped and crooked. It's odd, giving away money. You don't want someone thinking you pity them, though that's usually what it amounts to, and often for something so small—in this case, crooked glasses. Plus, having to go through airport security every morning just so you can work at McDonald's.

"Excuse me," I said. "This is going to sound crazy, but every day I choose someone to give fifty dollars to. Would you mind?" I put the bill on the counter in front of her and wondered for a moment if she hadn't misunderstood and thought I'd said fifty thousand.

"Oh my goodness!" she screamed like someone on a game show who'd just won an outsized prize—a boat stacked atop a BMW that's filled with diamonds and the exorbitantly priced ink cartridges my printer demands at the end of every fifth page. I raced away but could hear her behind me. "Did you see that? Fifty dollars! *Oh my God! Oh my God! Oh my God!*"

I guess I chose the right person, I thought as I hurried on to my gate, which was at the far end of the terminal. My flight wound up being delayed by half an hour, and I was hungry. Getting a snack meant walking by the McDonald's, and I didn't want the woman to see me again, so I just sat there and ate three raisins I found stuck to my check-book at the bottom of my tote bag. Oh, the price of saving people.

At an event that night, someone gave me a fifty-dollar bill. The following afternoon I handed it to a guy in his thirties who was eating out of a garbage can. He was strangely handsome and wore a headdress made from a pair of filthy trousers. It's embarrassing that my first thought wasn't *No one should have to live like that.* Instead, I wondered why I couldn't carry off a pants turban the way this guy could. *It isn't fair,* I said to myself, handing him the bill.

"God bless you," he muttered.

"Well, I don't know about that," I said.

At a bookstore in Salt Lake City later that week, someone gave me two five-dollar bills to hand out, and I thought, *Is that all?* The next day I was in Seattle and passed a man who was picking crushed cigarette butts off the sidewalk and lighting them. His fingertips had been blackened from dirt and fire. There was a convenience store not too far away, so I walked in and spent the ten dollars, plus three of my own, on a pack of Marlboros. "Here," I said, returning to where he was sitting on the filthy pavement. "Take these."

"Aaaahhh!" the man screamed and shielded his face, the way you might if you knew for a fact that someone was going to punch you in the nose.

"I'm not...," I said. "I'm trying to give you—"

"Aaaaaaaahhh!" He let out another cry, and passersby

looked my way, their expressions reading, *What's that monster in a skirt trying to do to that poor homeless person?*

But it wasn't a skirt. It was a pair of culottes!

"Aaaaahhh!"

"Oh, go to hell," I whispered. "I spent thirteen dollars on these cigarettes, and I don't even smoke anymore."

We must have been in front of a group home of some sort, for a moment later, a man who looked as troubled as the first—who was now rocking back and forth, still protecting his face with his hands—walked over and said in a too-loud voice, "I'll take them."

This fellow had greasy hair and was missing both his front teeth. The demanding part kind of bothered me, but he was clearly mentally ill, so he got a pass.

"Thank you," I said, and I handed him the cigarettes.

I continued to talk at my bookstore events about the fifty-dollar bills, hoping someone might be like the woman in Duluth, but no one stepped forward, and in time the subject was completely eclipsed by the things that men shove up inside themselves. If women come home from work and take their bras off, their husbands return and look for things they can force up their asses. In every city I was given a new example.

By the time a nurse told me about a patient who had inserted an electric toothbrush inside himself, and another who'd managed a two-liter bottle of Diet Mtn Dew, I was so inured that I said only, "Wait a minute. *Diet?*"

It wasn't my fault that the money theme faded. I put things

out there, and the audience chooses what it prefers to focus on. I think it was the mood the country was in. Something in the early summer of 2019 had us all thinking about enormous gaping assholes.

My final stop was in Reno. Then I went home to England as if none of this had ever happened. The only thing that stuck with me was that man in Seattle, the one who would rather pick crushed cigarette butts off the sidewalk than take the pack that I had bought for him, the one who cowered at my approach. I met so many people during that book tour. I shook hands. I asked questions. I connected. I'm not a bad man, honestly I'm not. So why do I worry he was the only person I encountered that month who truly saw me?

To Serbia with Love

You know when you're traveling with someone, and you realize too late that you're with the wrong person? That they, for example, want to stay at the cheapest place possible even though it's far from the center of town and is surrounded on either side by gas stations? Or perhaps they insist on taking the cut-rate flight that leaves from an airport you've never heard of and lands in a cornfield fifty miles from the city you were hoping to visit.

My friend Patsy is not that person. We have similar ideas on how to get to where we're going and where to stay once we arrive. We're of like mind as well when it comes to the length of our visit. The rule is that you have to stay the night in a country in order to cross it off your list, so usually that's our limit. Occasionally we'll spend two nights, but never any longer. This wouldn't work with someone who lives in the

United States. Who's going to fly twelve hours from Houston or Chicago in order to spend a day and a half in Moldova, of all places?

Patsy is American but lives in Paris, where she works as a tour guide. I'm in England but come to France every July and December for a periodontal appointment. In the summer, when it's hot, I'm in and out, but in the weeks before Christmas I take some extra time, and the two of us—me with freshly shredded, bleeding gums—go on a trip together. The first was to the Czech Republic, where we found ourselves in a muddy field, used tires and filthy stuffed animals laid out on the ground before us alongside wet boxes of rusty nails. "The internet said it was a flea market," Patsy said, her eyes filling with tears as she shivered in the early-morning cold. "This is *not* my fault, honestly it's not."

This happened in Warsaw as well, and Odessa, to name just a few places. The vendors in the countries we tend to go to are stocky women with scarves tied beneath their chins, and you don't dare catch their eyes. Doing so means beaming as they hold up a shorted-out curling iron with dried nail polish on it, or a crocheted blanket the color of sorrow. *Please don't unfold it,* Patsy and I think as the woman inevitably unfolds it, smiling to reveal three gold teeth in an otherwise empty mouth and saying, we can only imagine, "Look at how wretched my life is!"

OK, we think, reaching for our zlotys or dinars, our leva or lei or koruny, *who doesn't need a blanket?*

It would be all the more disappointing had we taken four

buses to reach the muddy field the flea market is always in, but we usually hire a driver—an extravagance but well worth it when you have only so much time. And they're always interesting people.

In Serbia it was a guy named Milos, who wore a big watch and had a scar on his face that ran from the corner of his mouth to his right ear. He was prompt and funny, and drove us from Belgrade to the small town of Bijeljina, just over the Bosnian border. Again and again he apologized for his English—needlessly, we thought. "My vocabulary, I worry, is very bad."

"In the last five minutes you've used the words *hooligan* and *pitiful,*" I reminded him. "Give yourself some credit, man!"

Milos's only drawback was that he couldn't talk to you without looking you straight in the eye—a problem, as he was in the front seat and we were in the back. Patsy, who is more prone to imagining worst-case scenarios than I am, felt certain that we would die in a head-on collision. I just thought we'd wind up paralyzed from the chins down.

It was worth it, though, to have things explained to us. Patsy and I went to Bosnia from Serbia, where we'd spent a night in Belgrade. "That means *White City,*" Milos told us at the start of our two-hour drive.

I'll say, I thought. Aside from some Chinese businessmen in our hotel, everyone I saw—everyone—was Caucasian. This is often the case in Eastern European countries no one wants to immigrate to. A few years back, in Romania, we were told about a Syrian man who arrived in Bucharest having walked eight hundred miles from Aleppo. When he learned that he was not in Austria, the refugee wept, put his blood-soaked shoes back on, and hit the road for Vienna.

"Two million Syrians came through Serbia," Milos told us, "but I don't think any of them stayed."

Outside the window, we saw a long banner hanging before a government building, with portraits of maybe a hundred fifty people on it, mainly men, all of them in their late teens or twenties.

"Were they killed in the war?" Patsy asked.

Milos looked over, then turned around to face us as he merged into another lane. "These are people which has been kidnapped by Albanians to have their inside parts stolen."

"Did they die?" I asked.

"Of course. Some butcher take their liver to sell to some alcoholic, maybe, and their kidneys to somebody else. The veins in their legs. Maybe some old smokers need their fresh lungs. All the parts that people might want were cut out and sold."

"That's called *harvesting*," I said, sounding, I feared, a little too much like an English teacher. "Their *organs* were *harvested*."

It would suck to be Albanian, as pretty much anywhere you go in the world, people will think poorly of you. It's like being a pirate. Whenever anything bad happens in Europe, when a young woman is discovered decomposing in a barrel or a child goes missing, Albanians are blamed. I thought their country was where you went to have your car or computer stolen.

Now, when Patsy and I eventually visit, we'll know to keep our eyes on our eyes as well.

Milos had been proud to be Yugoslavian. Being Serbian, though, was nothing special. He spoke with awe and reverence of Tito, the dictator who ruled the country until his death in 1980. "It meant something to have a Yugoslavian passport back then," he told us. "People saw it and said, 'Wow.' We had the third-biggest army in the world. We were powerful and respected." He pulled his Serbian passport from his jacket pocket and glared at it. "This, though, this is nothing."

It was Milos's dream that Yugoslavia, which started breaking apart in the nineties and is now divided into six separate republics, might be reunited and become communist again. "Life was better then," he told us. "Everybody was equal. Not like today, when you is having to work all the time to get ahead, and pay for this and that, which was all free back then."

In the West we're taught that people in former communist countries are joyful now, that anything is better than what they had before. Surprisingly, Milos was only thirty-five. He hadn't lived through Tito and had been just a boy when Yugoslavia started breaking up.

"But you can speak your mind now," Patsy reminded him. "You can read what you want and think for yourself."

Milos shrugged. "You think if I write something against the government today they is not going to be watching me and putting me on a list?"

"Maybe it's like if the United States broke apart," I said to Patsy that night over dinner. She's from Alabama, so she'd likely have to carry a passport with DIXIE written on it. Her flag would be the Confederate one, and Lynyrd Skynyrd would be the composer of her national anthem.

Patsy and I go to countries where people can still smoke in shops and restaurants and hotel lobbies; where cigarettes are cheap, but the packs have pictures on them of lungs that look barbecued, or of a little girl laying flowers on her mother's grave; where the group of eight at the breakfast table beside you all have lit Marlboros in their hands, or maybe six have Marlboros and two are sucking on cigars; places where, at the end of our short visits, all of our stuff smells like stale smoke—not just our coats and sweaters but even our keys and glasses. Our eyebrows probably stink as well.

And the breakfast rooms! In Odessa, beside the head cheese on the buffet there stood a bottle of vodka with glasses beside it. Eight a.m., and people were taking shots. The room looked like it had been decorated by Donald Trump. Curtains the shade and texture of pantyhose hung in limp swags over the windows. Chairs were high-backed and velvet, some gold and others the same pea green as the wallpaper. There were garish chandeliers overhead and, at our feet, a mosaic-tiled floor. Beside us, a man took cheesecake photos of the woman he was with. The way she posed, her breasts sticking out, her head tilted just so with a little rag of tongue showing, we felt we were intruding on something private. Looking on from the shadows were a number of bruisers, all stocky and thick-necked, wearing showy gold watches. The hair on their cheeks was the same length as the hair on their heads, like the legs on a fly.

"Who are those men who look like thugs?" Patsy asked the clerk at the front desk.

"Thugs," the woman answered. "They are here for your protection."

We go to places where thugs guard parked BMWs and stray dogs roam the streets, the bitches all with swollen teats. There are cats too, grease-covered from skulking beneath cars, one eye or sometimes both glued shut with pus.

I was told that in Romania there was a stray dog for every thirty-one people, but I saw hardly any the time Patsy and I went, at least not in Bucharest, the capital city. "We just shot them all," explained our driver. His name was Ion, and he picked us up at the airport. I greeted him with the Romanian I had spent the past month studying, and he said, in English, "OK. We go to the car then." Ion was nice-looking, maybe around five-nine, with a short stubble of hair.

"Do people tell you that you resemble James Franco?" I asked.

"Who is he?"

"An actor," I said. "Did you see *Rise of the Planet of the Apes,* or the one, I forget the title, where he cuts his own arm off?"

"I don't know it."

Ion's English was pretty good. Most of his mistakes had to do with verb tense: Plants were "putted" all over the place. A building "rised" in 1976. Referring to a missing mirror on his passenger-side door, he said, "It fell down" rather than "It fell off." No big deal. It was charming. I just didn't see why my baby Romanian couldn't be equally enchanting. "Girls are going to laugh at you when you talk," he warned.

On the way into town we passed a billboard for something called the DOVE BRAND DELUXE PRAWN RING, a wreath of jumbo shrimp with two different sauces puddled in the center. "Do you eat a lot of prawn rings in Bucharest?" I asked.

"That is the first time I have heard of one," Ion said. We were staying in a pedestrian zone, so he dropped us off at the edge of it and told us our hotel was one block straight ahead.

It was actually a half mile away. Most of the pass-ersby we stopped for directions didn't speak English, so my Romanian actually came in handy. "Go down two streets and take a left," people said. Just like in the audio program I had used.

The flea market in Bucharest was also in a field of mud. Ion waited with the car while Patsy and I walked around, surprised by all the human hair we saw. It wasn't stitched into wigs or falls but was just tied into bundles with string. I got the idea that it had been cut off without the owners knowing any-thing about it, perhaps at movie theaters or maybe when these people were sleeping. Look at it too intently, and the vendor would pick it up and wave it before your eyes. Patsy, who has beautiful red hair, actually sort of a deep orange color, tucked hers under her cap for safekeeping.

While we shopped, Ion got into a shouting match with a Gypsy. "Second time this month," he said as we climbed into the back seat. "The last one scratched my neck with her sharp, sharp fingernails!"

Sometimes our driver will act as a guide. This was the case in Lisbon, the only Western European city Patsy and I have visited together. We had a list of stores we wanted to go to, but at the end of every block, the driver, who was nearing seventy and was named Carlos, would pull over, saying, "David, I want you to look out your window to the left. There you will see a monument to Miguel Pouza, who was the first captain of tall ships to be presented to our queen in 1612. Next to him you will notice..."

Oh my God. I thought. *Is this really happening?*

"David and Patsy, I want you to get out of the car and cross the street. Look between those two buildings, and when you come back, I want you to tell me what you have seen."

At one point he showed us a bullfighting arena that had been turned into a mall. "As bad as people think it was, we never killed the bull in public view, the way they do in Spain. Instead, here in Portugal, we would do it backstage."

"Americans think that bullfighting is savage and backward, but if you could do it with firearms we'd probably be all over it," I said. "Can you imagine? The bull would be released and someone with a sawed-off shotgun would blow its front legs off."

Patsy can't bear to hear things like this. She's a vegetarian and won't even watch a movie if it has a weapon in it. Carlos, meanwhile, continued with his tour. "David, look straight ahead. Do you see those tiles?"

I noticed that he said *oosh-ul-lee* rather than *usually*. *Beach* was *bitch*, as in "Live in this mansion and you could have your own private bitch!"

"I do not care about your bitches," I wanted to tell him. "Or your churches or your famous sites. All I care about are your stores, so how about you just button your lip and drive me to the one I read about that sells the wax models of human intestines?"

I long ago stopped feeling bad about my interests. History? Give me a break! Culture? Yawn. Take me to the nearest supermarket!

When it came to drivers, I much preferred Ion's style. After a night in Bucharest, he collected Patsy and me at our hotel and drove us to Transylvania. As we got under way, I told him about a Frenchman I knew who often came to Romania to hunt.

"Yes, well, we have the biggest bear population in Europe," he said. "Sixty percent of them live right here, along with many foxes, boars, and lynxes, which are savage cats!"

The road we were on was lined on either side by grim cinder-block houses, which looked even worse beneath the heavy, pewter-colored sky. Villagers bundled in cheerless coats stood where the curbs would be if there had been curbs, some selling colossal onions and others staring mournfully into the oncoming cars.

"Do they want rides?" Patsy asked.

"Yes," Ion said.

"Feel free to pick someone up," I said.

"No way."

As we neared Transylvania we came upon villages that had likely been beautiful before the communist government put ugly concrete factories in the middle of them. In France they hide things like that, but here they were front and center, most shuttered now, with peeling paint and broken windows. The Carpathian Mountains surrounding us were magnificent, though, as were the pine forests. There was snow on the ground, and the boughs of the trees were heavy with it. It looked like a Christmas card, but with stray dogs rather than reindeer.

Ion suggested lunch at a ski resort, so we went to a place with sheepskins on the walls. The restaurant played Romanian music. It was mournful-sounding, and when I asked if the song we were listening to was related in any way to Christmas, Ion said yes.

"Is it about baby Jesus growing up only so that he could be nailed to a cross?"

"What gives you that idea?" he asked.

"It just sounds so tragic," I said, comparing it in my mind to, say, "Frosty the Snowman." It's surprisingly hard to identify other people's Christmas songs. Drivers are so helpful in this regard. Actually they're great for any kind of musical question.

"Who are some of your biggest pop stars?" I would ask years later in Milos's car as we neared the border between Serbia and Bosnia.

He thought for a moment, then offered up Zdravko Čolić. "He just did four sold-out concerts at our big sporting stadium and could have did even more."

"What are the names of some of his songs?"

"'Ej, draga draga' is one. That is meaning 'Hey, Baby Baby,' something like that. And 'Ti si mi u krvi,' which is 'You Are in My Blood.'"

"That's what I'm going to say when the border agent asks for my passport," I told him.

Milos turned around in his seat. "Oh, you better don't!"

In Bosnia, Patsy and I stayed in what amounted to a village of yesteryear. It really should have occurred to me that a hotel with barnyard animals, some roaming untethered and others—the goats, for instance—in pens, would also have roosters, and that they would start crowing right outside my authentic wooden hovel at four a.m. and continue until long after sunrise. We left the country exhausted, again in the company of Milos, who had driven from Belgrade to collect us. "Not to make you feel guilty, but it was your own government that destroyed Yugoslavia," he said. "Your CIA could not stand to see my country so powerful, and so they started a civil war to tear us apart."

Is this true? I wondered. On our last morning in Belgrade I'd been lectured at length by a man selling dish towels at a flea market. "We Serbs are not who your news media tells you we are," he began.

I wanted to say that our media tells us nothing about Serbs, or at least nothing that anyone pays attention to.

Most Americans can't identify Minnesota on a map, much less the former Yugoslavia. The man spoke of concentration camps and mass slaughters. He threw dates at me, and names. Patsy wandered over at one point and clearly wished she hadn't.

"Oh gosh," she said. "That's terrible."

"One thousand four hundred Serbs murdered in a day by one single Croat, who was then sent by your government to South America to fight the Russians. Women, children, old people: all of them cut at the throat with a knife like animals."

I wanted to say that the US government sending a Croatian war criminal to South America to help fight the Russians sounded ridiculous. Instead I only wished it sounded ridiculous. When I couldn't take it anymore, I picked up the dish towel I'd bought for the equivalent of seventy-five cents. "*Hvala,*" I called as I backed away from the table. This sounded like *fala* and was Serbian for *thank you.* "Easy to remember," I told Patsy, "because it's December, and a woman I met at a book signing once worked at a coffee shop where she was told to push the seasonal Fa La La La Latte."

Patsy's biggest fear, and perhaps her most irrational one, is that someone is going to shoot her in the head, execution-style. Thus, when we're in Ukraine or Moldova or Transnistria—the eerie disputed territory between those two countries—and a driver who looks like a thug and speaks little or no English pulls off the paved road onto a dirt one and stops,

I can feel her tense up beside me. She even slams her eyes shut.

"He's just turning around," I tell her, or, "It's OK. He only wanted to look at the map. Of where he's been instructed to bury our bodies."

I love hearing stories about the Americans Patsy guides through Paris. Or doesn't—a man, for instance, who canceled his trip when told he couldn't bring a gun into the Louvre.

"Why would he want to in the first place?" I asked.

"Exactly!" Patsy said.

Many of her clients get upset when they learn that things in France aren't exactly how they are in the United States, that you can't buy Big Gulps, for instance, or get A.1. Sauce for your steak frites. These are the ones who get down on their knees and kiss the ground when they disembark from their plane home to America.

What would they make of Bosnia and Moldova? I wonder. On the canceled visit we'd planned to North Macedonia, the hotel Patsy found for us included toilet paper on its list of amenities. Of course, not everywhere we go is like that. Estonia seemed to be doing fairly well, as did Lithuania and Latvia.

Paris is often in upheaval when we return from a trip. That was certainly the case in mid-December 2019. The government wanted to raise the retirement age from sixty-two to sixty-four, and the French people were not having it. Everyone was on strike, it seemed. Getting to town from the airport was a nightmare. Still, we had the feeling we were back at the center of the world. I felt the same way when I arrived in London a few days later, and when I continued on to Tokyo and Hong Kong and Sydney. The people I saw there felt it too. I didn't poll them; I could just tell. It was in their walk, in their appearance: *We matter!*

In many of the places that Patsy and I visit, the people don't have that certainty. I think of the Romanians standing at the side of the road, peering from their heavy-hooded coats at the oncoming traffic, and of the women with the scarves tied beneath their chins, packing up their unsold goods at the end of the day: the broken toaster ovens, the spotted tangerines. They never look particularly disappointed, as they never dare get their hopes up. I see these people and wonder what my life would be like had I not been lucky enough to be born where I was—for that's all it amounts to, dumb luck. What if my grandparents hadn't emigrated from their village in Greece, had been turned away because they didn't have health insurance or a college education, or enough money to meet some arbitrary new standard? Greece is just south of Albania, an easy trek for kidnappers. Would I still have my kidneys? My liver? Certainly, had my grandparents not immigrated, their only child—my father—could not have voted for Donald Trump.

In America, the talk now is all about white privilege, but regardless of your race, there's American privilege as well, or at least Western privilege. It means that when you're in Dakar or Minsk your embassy is open and staffed, and you don't need to hand out bribes in order to get what you need. That spark you feel when an idea comes to you—*This could work. I can actually make this happen!*—is Western privilege as well. It may not be certainty, but it's hope, and if you think that's worthless, try living in a place where nobody has it. Worse still, try getting a decent hotel room there.

The Vacuum

The supermarket closest to the apartment Hugh and I have on the Upper East Side of Manhattan isn't usually crowded. It doesn't deserve to be. The place isn't dirty or poorly stocked, just depressing, in part because the bulk of it is underground and windowless. Every now and then they'll hire a cheerful cashier, someone who acts as if she is getting paid and is not in fact shackled to the floor beneath her register, but the sunny ones never last long. I just shop there occasionally, and only because it's convenient.

In February 2020 I went to South America with my friend Dawn. There'd been talk about a virus in China, but I didn't give it much thought until I flew from Buenos Aires to Santiago and had my temperature taken while standing in the Chilean customs line. *Well, this is interesting,* I thought. It was the first time I'd seen one of those thermometers that look like a pistol, and I instinctively winced when the barrel was put to my forehead. *Is this what I'll do when someone actually shoots me execution-style?* I wondered. *Close my eyes and jerk a little?*

On the flight back to New York I noticed several of my fellow passengers wearing masks, and silently condemned them for overreacting, not realizing that by March my bare bottom would get more exposure to the sun than the lower half of my face would. The first sign I saw in the United States that things were falling apart was the grocery store I found so unpleasant. It had gone from zero to sixty in terms of customers, and seemingly overnight. Lines suddenly reached the rear wall, then snaked back to the registers. First to vanish was the toilet paper, followed by the most obvious toilet-paper substitutes: Kleenex, napkins, and paper towels. I remember looking long and hard at the coffee filters, thinking, *Too soon?*

Then went the food eaten by people who don't cook: frozen pizzas and burritos, pasta, spaghetti sauces in jars, and tuna.

There was a rumor that liquor stores might close, and that caused a run on vodka. Not the kind that came in slender frosted bottles and looked like awards for modern dance but the kind that came in jugs and might as well have a skull and crossbones on the label.

I tried to hoard-shop. On my first attempt, at a Whole Foods I had to wait in line to get into, I came away with two steaks and a pouch of dried coconut.

"*Coconut?*" Hugh said when I got home.

I pinched some out as if it were chewing tobacco and packed

it between my lower gum and cheek. "Well, I've seen you use it for cakes."

That evening, at another neighborhood supermarket, I tried again to hoard and returned home with a pint of buttermilk and some taco shells.

"I give up," Hugh said.

The following afternoon, really determined this time, I went with my sister Amy to a high-end store called Eataly. On that trip I came away with two sacks of Jordan almonds, a jar of anchovies, and a pack of hot dogs.

"You're pathetic!" Hugh said.

"Well, they're not just *any* hot dogs," I told him. "These are handcrafted by hot-dog artisans in"—I squinted at the label—"New Jersey."

Had I honestly just used the term *hot-dog artisans*? I said to Amy, "Sometimes don't you just hate yourself?"

She was no better at hoarding than I was—an outrage, given that we'd both grown up with our father, a professional when it came to stockpiling. I remembered him during the oil crisis of 1973, heading to the Shell station with empty cans and getting in line at four a.m. All our cars had a full tank, but he needed the next guy's ration as well. My sisters and I didn't even drive, but still he taught us how to siphon. I can clearly recall my first mouthful of gasoline, the shock of it, the wrongness. Spitting it onto the street, I'd thought, *Someone could have used that!*

"Can you imagine Dad twenty years younger?" I said to Amy after our failed trip to Eataly. "If he wasn't locked up in his assisted living facility, he'd have been first in line at his local Sam's Club, loading his forklift with pallets of canned sausages and fruit cocktail." How could we, his children, be so bad at the kind of shopping he prided himself on? Had we learned nothing? Our sister Lisa wasn't much better. "Bob and I heard they'd be getting some toilet paper in at Costco, but it was gone by the time we arrived."

"What do you mean, 'by the time we arrived'?" I could hear my father say. "You didn't spend the night camped outside the front door? You let someone else take what was rightfully yours?"

A little drugstore in my neighborhood had hand sanitizer one day. There was a sign in the window announcing it, and a number of people stood out on the sidewalk, looking at the sign and waiting for someone else to open the door. That happened a lot at first. No one wanted to touch the handle. "Fine," I'd always say, "*I'll* do it."

Then I'd have to stand there and let thirty customers through. Then twenty. Then ten. It was astonishing how quickly Manhattan emptied out. By mid-March my building was maybe a third full, and it got emptier still when it was decided that all work had to be suspended: no more carpenters or decorators. Then no more housekeepers or personal assistants. No more babysitters. No more furniture deliveries. Out on the streets, cabs disappeared. Stores closed or seriously curtailed their hours.

The only people who seemed to be working anymore were journalists. Just as I was certain that every aspect of the coronavirus had been exhausted, I found an article on how it was adversely affecting prostitutes. They couldn't exactly file for unemployment benefits, so many had apparently started GoFundMe campaigns.

When I mentioned the article to my agent, Cristina, she said, "I don't see why they can't just Skype. Not that it will really fix anything. It won't be long before sex robots drive all those people out of business."

Who are you? I wondered. I mean, sex robots! This was my agent!

There was also FaceTime, of course, which I supposed could be amended in this case to Sit-on-Your-Face Time.

A lot of people were moving their business online, though. Before everything went to hell, Amy had a trainer, a Pilates instructor, and a regular acupuncturist, all of whom suggested they continue their sessions virtually.

I said, "The first two make sense, but how would that work with the acupuncturist? Are you supposed to stick the needles in yourself?"

"He said we'd start by looking at my tongue and then talk about my general wellness for an hour," she told me. "I'd like to keep people in business, but this just leaves me feeling overwhelmed."

I'd already volunteered to run errands. Had one of my few remaining neighbors needed something from the supermarket or drugstore, I'd have been happy to fetch it. There were those who said that the best thing I could do for the people around me was to stay indoors. But I could take only so much isolation, and it wasn't like I was getting that close to anyone. When two people approached each other on the sidewalk now, they would hug opposite edges, like enemies. Our eyes didn't even meet anymore.

Often I'd slog down nineteen floors just to talk to the doorman. Together we'd look out at the street, at the traffic that wasn't there, and at the pedestrians who no longer walked by.

"Well, OK, then," I'd say after ten or so minutes. "I guess I'll go see what Hugh is up to."

Then I'd touch the elevator button with my elbow and head back upstairs, trying hard not to think about sex robots and how much one might possibly cost.

Before the pandemic, I thought my apartment needed to be vacuumed every other day, so, after lunch, no matter how busy I was, I'd roll up my sleeves and go at it. Now I realized it needed to be done *every* day—twice a day if I was spending a lot of time at my desk. My office chair has an old rattan seat that rains down dustlike shards when I sit for too long. These would get tracked from room to room when I refilled my coffee cup or pulled things out of the washing machine, which I'd recently learned had a special setting for towels.

Amy said, "Get the chair rewoven."

I said, "By whom?"

She said, "The blind."

But the blind weren't in their workshops now. And who

could blame them? Since the shelter-in-place order, I'd noticed twice the usual amount of shit on the streets. I reckoned that, because there was nobody around to yell at dog owners, they thought, *Why bother picking it up?* Or else they were using the virus as an excuse, acting as if they had to get back indoors right away, like another thirty seconds was going to get them killed. And who would be stepping in all this extra shit? The blind, that's who!

Still, I offered to walk a dog for anyone too frightened to go out. Then I amended it and said I'd be willing to walk any dog that had a colostomy bag. I mean, really, I had to draw the line somewhere.

"What you're doing," Hugh told me, "is killing time." And, of course, he was right. Vacuuming, dusting, torturing my towels with three-hour wash cycles: it was all just busywork until the sun set and the clock eventually—finally—struck midnight. Then I'd put a few dollars in my pocket and sneak outside to a New York I'd never imagined, one in which I was, if not the only person, then at least just one of a chosen few.

Here is a random night, plucked out of hundreds: I'd just walked six miles and had crossed paths with no one. With no traffic to stop me, the only time I'd paused was to read a sign someone had put in the window of a padlocked bar: I USED TO COUGH TO HIDE A FART. NOW I FART TO HIDE A COUGH. I copied the words down in my notebook, then turned a corner to find a man with a black eye and a fistful of potato chips standing in the middle of the sidewalk. "Do you speak English?" he asked.

I learned years ago never to stop. It sounds heartless, I know, but whether it's a guy with a black eye or one of those young people with a clipboard, the moment you engage, you're finished. I'd been with my sister a few months earlier when a woman holding a cardboard sign said, "Can I ask you a question?"

"Aries," Amy called over her shoulder as we sped by.

The man with the black eye said as I passed that they wouldn't let him on the subway unless he had another dollar, so I gave it to him, even though there were no more trains at that hour. It wasn't generosity that caused me to turn around. I just wanted a closer look at his face.

Did you at least fight back? I wanted to ask. The area surrounding his black eye was swollen, and I noticed some blood on his shirt.

"I just want to get home, man," he said.

"Me too," I told him. But in truth I still had a few miles in me. The lockdown was brutal for people with Fitbits, especially those who lived under curfews. I had a perfect record stepwise and was not about to break it for a raging pandemic.

If I was out after midnight, when the streets were deserted, I failed to see how I was endangering anyone. It was creepy, though, the emptiness. If I were driving through the city, looking for someone to rob, I'd have definitely chosen myself—who wouldn't have? I'm small. I was always alone and keeping to the shadows like a rat, which I was seeing a lot of. Forty or fifty of them some evenings, especially when the garbage bags were heaped on the curb. They'd spill out as I passed, almost on cue, a finishing touch to the general sense of doom and societal decay I was already feeling.

There were troubling sights in the daytime as well: a couple shooting up heroin on Fifth Avenue. They were seated on the ground, their backs against the facade of a shop that only two months earlier had been open and likely selling $4,000 crocodile panty shields. I looked at the two, and they looked back as if to say, *And...?*

Walking home from Amy's apartment to my own sometime later, I came upon a scowling blast furnace of a man who had built a little encampment beneath a scaffold and surrounded himself with handwritten signs, one of which read, FUCK YOU DIAPER FACE.

Normally in New York one out of every two hundred people you pass is crazy. Now it felt more like one out of every two. I was in Times Square late one Sunday night. It was deserted, and I came upon a man in a wheelchair who was pushing himself along with his feet. "Look at the fucking clown!" he shouted.

I glanced down at what I was wearing and thought, *What's wrong with a mechanic's jacket that falls to my ankles?*

"Fucking clown!" the man bayed again. I followed his eyes and saw...an actual clown, with a red nose and turquoise hair, standing on the other side of Broadway. *Well, all right then,* I thought.

My neighborhood is known for its old rich people and, subsequently, its hospitals. The closest of them now had a refrigerated truck parked outside in which dead bodies were being stored. Sirens wailed around the clock. Looking back, I can't believe that I never got sick. Hugh, Amy, and I flew fairly often to North Carolina. There, we'd wave at my father through the window of his locked-down assisted living center. A quick stop for coffee and we'd continue on to Emerald Isle, where the coronavirus was widely thought to be a hoax, and unmasked people looked at you the same way that New York heroin addicts did, as if to say, *Yeah, and what the fuck are you going to do about it?*

It wasn't strangers I was worried about, though. If COVID were to get me, it would have come from a friend or acquaintance. Throughout the height of the pandemic, Hugh and I had dinner parties—at least two a week, and sometimes up to four. When questioned, I'd explain that the guests we invited were members of our bubble. But it wasn't true. Anyone willing to leave their house was welcome. We ate a lot of ground water buffalo those first few months. That was the only thing I managed to successfully hoard. There was a stand that sold it at the Union Square farmers' market, and I'd come home once a week with a good five pounds' worth.

"What am I supposed to make with *this*?" Hugh asked the first time I presented him with it.

I'd posed the same question to the vendor. "Use your imagination," he told me.

So I said to Hugh, "Use your imagination."

We had water buffalo moussaka, water buffalo Bolognese, grape leaves stuffed with water buffalo—even water buffalo enchiladas.

It sounds petty, but if at any time during the meal a dinner guest used the word *surreal* to describe our current situation, or the phrase *hunkered down,* I would make a mental note to disinvite them from any future get-togethers. I hated the clichés that came with the pandemic, hated hearing *the new normal.* Oh, and *heroes.* At first the word was used for health-care professionals. Then for essential workers. Then we were *all* heroes. "Give yourself a great big hand, and stay safe!"

More irritating still was the new spirt of one-downsmanship that seemed to have taken hold. A year earlier, had I written in an essay, "I woke up and washed my face," no one would have thought anything of it. Now, though, I would immediately be attacked as tone deaf and elitist.

"Oh, how nice that you can just 'wake up and wash your face,'" someone would write in the comment section or tweet. "And in New York, no less! I, meanwhile, don't even *have* a face anymore. I had to sell it so I could feed my family during the *worldwide pandemic* you obviously never heard about. Now, when I try to eat, the food falls onto my lap because I don't have any cheeks to keep it in my mouth with. Think of *that* when you're holding your washcloth, you fucking privileged prick!"

A previously beloved talk show host began broadcasting from her home, and people went nuts. "Hold on a minute, she lives in a mansion!"

"Well, yes," I wanted to say. "A mansion bought with money that *you* gave her."

Everyone was angry and looking for someone to blame:

Trump, Fauci, China, Big Pharma. This had to be somebody's fault. "Back off!" a certain type of person would snarl if you stood only five feet and eleven inches away from them.

"Your mask isn't completely covering your nose," a middle-aged woman informed a much older one in my neighborhood Target one afternoon. "Miss," she called a second later to the cashier, "Miss, her mask isn't completely covering her nose!"

It was a golden era for tattletales, for conspiracy theorists, for the self-righteous. A photographer came one afternoon to take my picture. I was standing in the middle of East 70th Street, posing as instructed, when a woman with silver hair approached. She was on the sidewalk, a good twenty feet away, but still she felt the need to scold me. "Cover your face!" she screeched.

"Oh, for God's sake, this is for the *Times*!" I shouted back.

I saw a guy in a T-shirt that read, DEADLIEST VIRUS IN AMERICA: THE MEDIA.

I saw a woman in a T-shirt that read, YOU'D LOOK BETTER WITH A MASK ON.

"You know who I hate?" I said to Amy over water buffalo Swedish meatballs that night. "Everyone."

When the vaccines came along, we all pounced. "I'll take whatever you've got and as soon as possible."

In late spring 2021, it was announced that we no longer had to wear masks on the streets of New York. I lowered mine to below my nose. The next day I carried it in my hand, and from then on in my pocket, at the ready should I enter a store, my fitness center, or the lobby of my building—any place that asked it of me. Hugh continued to wear his outdoors long after it was no longer required. When I asked why, he shrugged. "It's just easier."

In the course of a week, New York returned to itself. Not completely—theaters and concert halls hadn't yet reopened—but people crept back from wherever it was they'd been hiding. There was traffic, and you could easily find a taxi again. As the sidewalks became crowded, I thought, *Oh no. Now I hate people even more than I did during the lockdown!* How had I forgotten about pedestrians who walk and text at the same time, or dog owners who block your path with their extendable leashes so that their pit bull mix can sniff the ass of someone else's, and both owners can say, with great virtue and often simultaneously, "He's a rescue!"

Neighbors who had decamped to the Hamptons for a year wondered why this or that particular business had gone under.

"Um, because you weren't here to support it?"

Given all the things that disappeared, I was surprised by what survived. I went into a long-shuttered store one afternoon looking for a gift for Hugh's nephew, and the salesperson said, "Welcome in."

"Really?" I said. "*That* endured—'Welcome in'?" I'd hoped it might have been forgotten, or consigned to the past like "Howdy-do." I can't stand "Welcome in."

"You don't need the *in* part," I've said to salesclerks more times than I can count. Then I become the crank who's correcting people about their grammar.

*   *   *

The terrible shame about the pandemic in the United States is that more than nine hundred thousand people have died to date, and I didn't get to choose a one of them. How unfair that we lost Terrence McNally but not the guy on the electric scooter who almost hit me while he was going the wrong way on Seventh Avenue one sweltering afternoon in the summer of 2021. Just as I turned to curse him, he ran into a woman on a bicycle who had sped through a red light while looking down at her phone. Both of them tumbled onto the street, the sound of screeching brakes all around them, and I remembered, the way you might recall a joyful dream you'd once had, that things aren't as bad as they sometimes seem, and life can actually be beautiful.

Pearls

It's July in West Sussex, and I'm at a garden party, talking with a lawyer who has two sons in their early twenties. The oldest is living in Scotland, and the other, a sullen college student, is home for the month, tearing everyone's head off. "So, do *you* have children?" she asks.

"Oh no," I tell her. "Not yet anyway. But I *am* in a relationship."

She says that she is glad to hear it.

"My boyfriend will turn twenty-one this coming Wednesday," I continue, "and you are so right about the moodiness of young men his age. I mean, honestly, what do they have to be so angry about?"

I do this all the time—tell people misleading things about Hugh. It's fun watching them shift gears as they reevaluate who they think I am. Sometimes I say that he's been blind since birth or is a big shot in the right-to-life movement, but the best is when he's forty-plus years my junior.

"Well...good for you," people say while thinking, I'm pretty sure, *That poor boy!* Because it's creepy, that sort of age difference—vampiric.

"There's a formula for dating someone younger than you," my friend Aaron in Seattle once told me. "The cutoff," he explained, "is your age divided by two plus seven." At the time, I was fifty-nine, meaning that the youngest I could go, new-boyfriend-wise, was thirty-six and a half. That's not a jaw-dropping difference, but although it might seem tempting, there'd be a lot that someone under forty probably wouldn't know, like who George Raft was, or what hippies smelled like. And, little by little, wouldn't those gaps add up and leave you feeling even older than you actually are?

It's true that Hugh is younger than I am, but only by three years. Still, I thought he'd never reach sixty. Being there by myself—officially old, the young part of old, but old nevertheless—was no fun at all. *C'mon,* I kept thinking. *Hurry it along.* His birthday is in late January, which makes him an Aquarian. This means nothing to me, though my sister is trying her damnedest to change that. Amy's astrologer predicted that Biden would win the 2020 presidential election, and when he did, she offered it as proof that Rakesh—that's his name, Rakesh—has extraordinary powers and thus deserves not just my respect but my business.

"You have to make an appointment and at least *talk* to him," she said.

"No, I don't," I told her. "I mean, my dry cleaner predicted the same thing. Lots of people did."

I'm a Capricorn, and according to the astrologer Lisa Stardust my least compatible signs for dating are Aries and Leo. My best bets are Cancers, Scorpios, and Pisceans.

I haven't looked at what astrological signs Hugh should avoid going out with, mainly because it's irrelevant. Not long after he turned sixty-one, we celebrated our thirtieth anniversary. Will we make it to thirty-five years? To fifty? Either way, do I really need to hear about it from Rakesh?

My mother became interested in astrology in the nineteen eighties. She wasn't a kook about it; she simply started reading the horoscopes in the *Raleigh News & Observer*. "Things are going to improve for you financially on the seventeenth," she'd say over the phone, early in the morning if the prediction was sunny and she thought it might brighten my day. "A good deal of money is coming your way, but with a slight hitch."

"Oh, no!" I'd say. "Are you dying?" I thought it was hooey, but in the back of my mind, a little light would always go on. I guess what I felt was hope—my life would change, and for the better! The seventeenth would come and go, and although I'd be disappointed, I would also feel vindicated: "I *told* you I wouldn't find happiness."

She never had her chart done, my mother, but she did branch out and start reading the horoscopes in *Redbook* and in *Ladies' Home Journal,* a magazine that had come to our home for as long as I could remember. The only column in it that interested me, the only one I regularly read, was called Can This Marriage Be Saved?

You could have taken everything I knew about long-term relationships back then and fitted it into an acorn cap. I thought that, in order to last, you and your wife or boyfriend or whatever had to have a number of mutual interests. They didn't need to be profound. Camping would qualify, or decoupaging old milk cans. The surprise is that sometimes all it takes is a mutual aversion to overhead lights, or to turning the TV on before eleven p.m. You like to be on time and keep things tidy, the other person's the same, and the next thing you know thirty years have passed and people are begging you to share your great wisdom. "First off," I say, "never, under any circumstances, look under the hood of your relationship. It can only lead to trouble." Counseling, I counsel, is the first step to divorce.

I've thought of that *Ladies' Home Journal* column a lot lately, wondering if marital problems in the seventies and eighties weren't all fairly basic: She's an alcoholic. He's been sleeping with his sister-in-law. She's a spendthrift and a racist, he's a control freak, etc.

No couple argued over which gender their child should be allowed to identify as; no one's husband or wife got sucked into QAnon or joined a paramilitary group. Sure, there were conspiracy theories, but in those pre-internet days it was harder to submerge yourself in them. A spouse might have been addicted to Valium but not to video games, or online gambling. I don't know that one can technically be addicted to pornography, but that's bound to put a strain on marriages, especially now, when it's at your fingertips, practically daring you *not* to look at it.

I've watched a number of movies and TV shows lately in which the characters' marriages dissolve for no real reason. I said to Hugh during *Ted Lasso,* "Did I miss the episode where he or his wife had an affair?" The same was true of Noah Baumbach's *Marriage Story:* "*Why* are they getting a divorce?"

Don't people who feel vaguely unfulfilled in their relationships just have too much time on their hands? Decide that you need to discover your true, independent self, and the next thing you know you'll be practicing Reiki or visiting an iridologist. That, I've learned, is someone who looks deep into your eyes and can see your internal organs. My sister Amy went to one, who told her that she had something stuck in her colon.

She took the diagnosis to her acupuncturist, who said that, actually, what the iridologist had seen in my sister's eyes was trauma.

Amy said, "Trauma?"

He said, "Remember you told me you saw a mouse *and* a water bug in your kitchen one day last month?"

She said, "Yes."

He said, "That's trauma."

My sister is not dating anyone—a good thing, as she's got way too much time on her hands. And that, I think, is the number one reason so many relationships fail. Too much free time, and too much time together. I'm normally away from

Hugh between four and six months a year, and when the pandemic canceled the tours I had scheduled, I panicked. We were in New York at the time, so I sought out his old friend Carol. "What's he really like?" I asked her. "I think I sort of knew once, but that was twenty-five years ago."

Trapped together for months on end, I learned that Hugh reads a lot. Like, every word of the *Times,* the *Washington Post,* and the *New York Review of Books.* Oddly, though, he doesn't seem to retain much. Whenever guests came to dinner and the talk turned to politics, Hugh, who might have delivered an informed opinion on, for example, Trump's proposed withdrawal from the WHO, would say, "I think we should line them all up and shoot them."

"Shoot who?" I'd ask, though I knew the answer.

"All the jerks who think we should withdraw."

That's his family's most damning epithet: jerk.

"Yes, well, that's not going to happen," I'd tell him. "It's not a real solution to the problem."

"Then I don't want to talk about it."

When not reading or cooking, Hugh goes to his studio and stares out the window, high on paint fumes, I'm guessing. I've never known anyone who can stand still as long as he does, moving nothing but his eyes, which shift back and forth like a cat's on one of those plastic wall clocks where the swinging tail is the pendulum. He doesn't listen to music while he's in there, or to the radio. Once, I put on a recording of Eudora Welty reading a number of her short stories, and, though he claimed to enjoy it, after "Petrified Man" he said he didn't want to hear any more. He likes to be alone with his thoughts, but me, I can't think of anything worse.

When not reading or cooking or staring out his window at nothing, Hugh practices piano. He started taking lessons on a rented upright when he was ten and living in Ethiopia, but his father couldn't bear to hear him practice. He wasn't particularly inept, but noise, any noise, bothered his dad, a novelist with a day job as a diplomat. Then the family moved to Somalia, where pianos were hard to come by, not to mention piano teachers, and his father wrote another book.

After a fifty-year break, Hugh started taking lessons again, this time on a baby grand a friend gave him, and though he's really committed, it always sounds to me like he just started last week. "I can't play when you're in the room," he told me. "I feel judged."

Then he decided that he couldn't play when I was in the apartment.

And so we bought the apartment upstairs from us.

"So that you'll have somewhere to go when he *practices piano?*" asked Amy, who bought the apartment upstairs from her just so she could get away from her rabbit.

"Exactly," I told her.

"Makes sense," she said.

I'm up there all the time now. We have no interior staircase connecting the two places, so Hugh emails me when he's got news. "Lunch is ready." "The super is here to fix your closet door." That type of thing. We took ownership just as New York went into lockdown, and furniture deliveries were banned in our building. Luckily, the previous owner agreed to leave a sofa and a bed. I found a few chairs on the street, a folding table, a bucket I could overturn and use as a footstool. For months, it looked like a twelve-year-old's clubhouse. Not that we didn't both spend time there. Hugh can do everything upstairs that he does downstairs except practice piano. We call the second apartment Luigi's. "Will we be having dinner on the nineteenth floor or up at Luigi's?"

Luigi's, we decided, is for casual dining.

Eventually we moved our bedroom to the second apartment. After thirty years together, sleeping is the new having sex. "That was amazing, wasn't it!" one or the other of us will say upon waking in the morning.

"I held you in the night."

"No, I held *you!*"

"You kids think you invented sleep," I can imagine my mother saying.

But didn't we? Hugh and I try new positions. ("You got drool on my calf!") We engage in quickies (naps). Three times a week I change the sheets so that our bed will feel like one in a nice hotel. Pulling back the comforter, we look like a couple in a detergent commercial. "Smell the freshness!"

For a thirtieth anniversary, you're supposed to offer pearls, but instead, for roughly the same price, I went to the Porthault shop on Park Avenue and got Hugh a set of sheets. The "Fabric Care" section on the company's website reads, in part, "Do not overload the dryer, as your linens need room to dance."

How did we become these people? I wonder.

Hugh says that if we ever get separate bedrooms, that's it—he's finished. I know this works for a lot of couples, they're happy being down the hall from each other, but I couldn't bear such an arrangement. "This is what I'll miss after you're dead," I tell him as I turn out the light, meaning, I guess, the sensation of being dead together.

Hugh might be a mystery to me, but it's a one-way street. "I'm sorry," I'll often say to him.

"That's all right."

"What was I apologizing for?" I'll ask.

"Telling the doorman that my mother looks like Hal Holbrook," he'll say, or "Wishing I would get COVID just so you could write about it."

He nails it every time!

I didn't need to tell him that after we're all vaccinated and theaters reopen, he will never see me again. "I've asked my agent to book me solid—I'll do three hundred and sixty-five shows in a row, take a night off, and then start all over again," I said. "I want to make up for lost time, and then some."

He accuses me of being money hungry, and I wish it were that simple. Honestly, it's the attention I'm after.

"What about me?" he asks. "Doesn't *my* attention matter?"

I say that he doesn't count, though of course he's one of a handful of people in my life—along with my sisters, my cousins, and a couple of old friends—who actually *do* count. I just don't necessarily need him by my side every moment that I'm awake. Sometimes it's enough to press my ear against the living-room floor of the upstairs apartment and faintly hear him practicing piano down below, frowning at the keys, I suspect, and at the music before him, a boy again. So determined to get it right.

Fresh-Caught Haddock

When George Floyd was killed and seemingly overnight all of New York came to smell like fresh plywood, I thought of Schenectady.

"Why there?" my sister Amy asked. She was with Hugh and me on the terrace of our apartment on the Upper East Side of Manhattan. From where we stood, we could hear the roiling cauldron twenty stories below us: sirens, shouting, the distant sounds of breaking glass—all blended together into a furious, muffled roar.

"Years ago I was on a plane, seated next to a middle-aged Black woman who was reading a Bible," I began. "I was working a crossword puzzle and said to the flight attendant—a white guy, not just gay but a queen—'Excuse me, but do you know how to spell *Schenectady*?'

"He told me that he had no idea, and just as I was sort of

hating him for it, the woman with the Bible said, 'S-c-h-e-n-e-c-t-a-d-y.' She spelled it with her eyes shut, maybe to prove that she wasn't cheating."

Amy spat an olive pit into her palm. "Oops."

"Exactly," I said. "Why hadn't I turned to her in the first place? I told myself I'd asked the flight attendant because it was his job to serve me, but how true was that, really? Did I ask him because he was white or because he wasn't reading a Bible?"

"What does that have to do with anything?" Amy asked.

I shrugged. "I guess I don't think that people who read Bibles on planes are all that smart."

"I don't know that being smart really plays into it," Amy said. "I'm sure there are plenty of dummies in Schenectady who have no problem spelling their town's name. I mean, it's part of their address." She dropped the olive pit into a planter Hugh had just filled with pansies. "I can't spell *Minneapolis* or *Minnesota*. Does that make me stupid?"

I said, "Yes."

She sighed. "I know. I'm an idiot."

Hugh headed indoors to make fresh drinks for himself and Amy. "I could have spelled *Schenectady* for you."

"Yes, well, you weren't there, were you?" I said. "You're never there when I really need you."

He and I had just returned from two weeks at the Sea Section. The New York we'd left behind us had already been changed by COVID-19, but now that we'd returned, it felt doubly different. For the first time since February, the virus was no longer the only news: the unrest was. The country had gone from one massive headline story to another, and it felt like anything might happen next: a cataclysmic natural disaster, an alien invasion. If I was overreacting, it was because New York had borne a bigger brunt of the year 2020 than many other places—North Carolina, for instance.

"The coronavirus never happened on Emerald Isle," I told Amy. "Or, OK, it *almost* didn't happen. At the grocery stores hardly anyone had a mask on. Same at the Dairy Queen. Coming from Manhattan, where we can't leave the house without our faces covered, it was a real..." I'd planned to say *shock,* but what came out instead was *vacation.*

"I want to go," Amy said. And so we made plans to return in a few weeks with her and her friend Adam. In the meantime, shops were being looted, and there were almost nonstop local protests, the moods of which varied from peaceful to confrontational. Five months earlier, I'd been in Hong Kong and asked people about the pro-democracy demonstrations there, surprised to learn that if you lived in certain parts of town and avoided your television, you could easily know nothing about them. That was certainly not the case in New York, where, no matter your neighborhood, the protests were impossible to ignore.

I walked downtown the day after Amy came for dinner, and fell upon a crowd that had gathered in Union Square. A number of people had signs, but before I could make them out, I was stopped by a young woman with green hair who wanted to hand me a plastic bottle.

"Water, sir?"

I shook my head no.

"How about some hand sanitizer? Or I have chips if you need a little something to eat." I guessed that she was a college student and assumed she was selling these things. But no, it seemed they were free.

"That's all right, but thanks," I said.

The crowd at the southern edge of the park wasn't doing anything in particular. Some of the people who had signs were hoisting them with no apparent sense of urgency in the direction of the police, who formed a ragged line on the other side of 14th Street, talking among themselves. Protest-wise, it seemed a good place to get started, so I went to Amy's and returned with her half an hour later, noting as we wandered into the throng, "We look like we're searching for our children."

Grandchildren was probably more like it, as we were by far the oldest people I saw.

"Water?" an earnest woman with pigtails asked. "Do you want some pretzels? Something to get your blood sugar up?"

"Need a list of all the local bathrooms?" another student-aged person asked, offering me a clearly marked map. This was nothing like what the TV news had been showing. Here there were no crowbars, just candy bars. And chips and Cheetos and dried fruit slices. "Are you *sure* I can't give you a little something to eat?" asked a dogged young snacktivist.

I reckoned there were maybe three hundred people in the park. Signs included WHITE SILENCE NO MORE, DEFUND NYPD,

NO EXCUSE 4 ABUSE, and BLM, an abbreviation for *Black Lives Matter*. A person I couldn't see was beating a drum, and while it felt like something should kick off, nothing did. Every so often applause would break out, though I was never sure why.

"It's just a gathering, really," the young woman standing next to me explained. She had a ring in her nose, and like most everyone around us, she was white.

It's an odd spot to occupy—the ally. On some website that morning, I'd watched a video of two identical-looking blondes spray-painting I CAN'T BREATHE on the facade of a Starbucks in Los Angeles.

"What are you *doing*?" a Black protester shouted. "That's something *I'm* going to get blamed for. *My* people. Who asked for your help anyway?"

The girls stopped but only because they were finished. In another video, a white guy with silver hair was using a pick—the sort gold miners hoist in movies—to break up paving stones he could hurl at the police.

A Black protester intervened, saying, much like the woman in L.A. had, that *he* was going to get blamed for it. But the guy with the pick continued until he was tackled to the ground by the Black fellow and a few of his friends, who subsequently delivered him to the very cops he'd intended to stone.

I thought I'd support the movement the way I had become accustomed to: by donating money and then telling people I'd donated twice as much. The moment I sent off my contributions, I saw the protests differently, for now I had done something and could feel superior to those who hadn't.

*   *   *

In the early days of the protests there was looting, and the news coverage made me anxious. My fear was that my favorite stores would be emptied and that when the city finally opened back up again after the COVID restrictions there'd be nothing left for me to buy. Amy shared my concern, so we left Union Square and walked to SoHo, where two of the shops we most cared about were located. Both were boarded up, but I wasn't sure if that was preventive or the result of smashed windows.

"It's not like I really *need* anything," I said sulkily as we headed back uptown. Neither of us had ever gone so long without shopping—close to a hundred days, it had been—and I wasn't quite sure who I was anymore. When my agent's birthday rolled around, I wound up giving her two bottles of wine and a gift card from a pharmacy she likes. "Those are, like, presents that *Lisa* would come up with," I said to Amy. She's not necessarily cheap, our sister, just unimaginative.

There were just so many questions I wanted answered. How, for instance, did people find the shoe style they were looking for, let alone the proper size, when looting big Nike stores? "You're an amateur wandering around a massive, probably dark stockroom with ten minutes at most, while the salesclerks, who are pros, seem to need *twice* that amount of time," I said to Amy.

Just then we ran into a protest march, an actual moving one. It was heading our way—west on Houston Street—so we joined it. Again, it was hard to estimate the crowd size. A thousand people? More? Social distancing was in practice, sort of, and most everyone I saw had the lower half of their face covered. In this particular case I actually welcomed my mask, as it relieved some of the pressure of chanting, which is something I've never been comfortable with. It's the same with prayer and the Pledge of Allegiance. I even lip-synch "Happy Birthday," so I was glad that my mouth was obscured and no one could see whether or not I was joining in.

"Hey, hey / Ho, ho / Racist cops have got to go!" the crowd shouted as Amy and I merged into it. This template has been around since the nineteen fifties and has to be my least favorite. True, it can be easily tailored to any cause, but you always know the word that's going to rhyme with *ho* will be *go*. It's lazy.

Next came "Whose streets?"

"Our streets!"

Then it was "NYPD, suck my dick."

I'm not sure how I feel about that one. *Is someone performing fellatio on you* really *the greatest punishment you can imagine?* I wanted to ask. I was thinking they might change it to "NYPD, kiss my ass," but that has its place as well. "Eat me out"? "Drink my piss"? Anything sexual is going to step on someone's toes.

"Black Lives Matter!" followed "Suck my dick!" and then we were back to "Whose streets? Our streets!" It's always interesting to watch a chant die, like a match going out. Some can burn for decent stretches of time, but with this crowd there appeared to be a strict forty-five-second policy.

Everyone seemed to have their phones out, and I noticed a lot of people taking selfies. This struck me as vulgar, but what *isn't* a background for an Instagram post anymore? I know that people are now taking pictures of themselves at funerals, because when I looked up "selfies at...," "...funerals" was the third option Google gave me. I clicked on it, aghast to find mourners posing beside the caskets of their dead friends and relatives. Some people had their thumbs up, meaning...what exactly? Great embalming job? Great death?

The march moved west and then turned north onto LaGuardia Place. It bottlenecked at Washington Square Park, so Amy and I took our leave. I walked her home and then continued on foot to my place, another fifty-three blocks north.

As the days passed and the marches became ubiquitous, I grew to think of them much the way I do about buses and subways. *I'll just take this BLM down to 23rd Street.* The people were friendly, the snacks plentiful, and it felt good to walk in the middle of the avenue.

At 23rd I might wait an hour or so before catching another BLM back home, or crosstown to the West Side. While marching, I'd look at the people around me and wonder what they were thinking. It's like at the symphony. I always assumed that the audience was comparing this rendition of, say, Mahler's Second to a superior one. Then I started asking around and learned that people were entertaining the same crazy thoughts I was: *How long would it take me to eat all my clothes—not the zippers and buttons but just the fabric? If I had to do it in six months, could I? If you shredded a sport coat very finely and added half a cup to, say, stuffing, would your body even notice it?*

I felt sure that while marching everyone around me thought of racism and of the many Black Americans who have been killed by the police over the years. We who were white likely considered our own complicity, or, rather, we touched on it briefly—that exposed wire—before moving on to other people who were much worse than we were. But then the time stretched on, and our thoughts strayed, didn't they?

Something I thought of one afternoon, marching uptown with a sizable crowd, was a well-known movie actor who had contacted me almost thirty years earlier when Hugh and I lived in SoHo. He wanted me to come by his house to discuss a possible collaboration, and I was flattered, for I had never met anyone famous. It was snowing, and almost three feet had accumulated by the time I left my apartment. The actor didn't live far from me, half a mile, maybe, but getting to his house was a real pain given my short legs and the waterproof boots I didn't have.

I arrived to find his two young children—a boy and a girl—in the dining room, being served by a thin Black woman whose hair was covered with a do-rag. She said hello to me as we passed by, and I noticed the steam coming off the soup she was setting down.

"You're lucky she came in to work in weather like this," I

said to the actor as we made our way to the living room. "And on a Saturday, no less!"

He offered a thin smile. "Actually, that's my wife."

My face still burns to think of this, but if nothing else, it taught me a lesson. From that day on, whenever I go to someone's home and see a person of a different race working either inside or outside the house, I say, "Is that your husband?" or "How come you make your wife do all the cleaning?"

They always answer, "Conchita, my *wife*? She's, like, twenty years older than me and has four kids! Plus I'm already married. To a man." Eventually, though, I'll be right, and my host will say, "May I just thank you for being the *one* person in my life who's not a horrible racist?"

As the weeks passed, I saw more and more protest signs reading DEFUND THE POLICE. *That won't be doing us much good come election time,* I thought, worried over how this would play on Fox News: "The left wants it so that when armed thugs break into your house and you dial 911, you'll get a recording of Rich Homie Quan laughing at you!"

Amy worried too. It wasn't taking money allocated for law enforcement and redirecting it toward social services that bothered her—rather, it was the language and how Trump would use it to scare people. He'd already started, and I imagined that, leading up to the election, he would just keep hammering at it.

"Then there are all the statues being pulled down," Amy said when she and Adam arrived on Emerald Isle. "I'd thought that would be nearly impossible, that they were, like, screwed into the ground or something, but I guess all you need is some good rope and a dozen or so really mad people."

"Mad *strong* people," Adam added.

"I'm not sure the general public really pays all that much attention to statues," I said. "Don't you think you could come in the night and replace General Braxton Bragg's head with that of, say, Whoopi Goldberg, and it would take months for anyone to notice? Don't most of us see a bronze figure on a pedestal and think, simply, *Statue?*"

Amy guessed that I was right.

"For those few exceptions who pay closer attention, you could keep the monument and change the plaque," I said. "It could read something like CHESTER BEAUREGARD JR.—UNFORTUNATE BLACKSMITH WHO BORE A STRIKING RE-SEMBLANCE TO THE TRAITOR GENERAL BRAXTON BRAGG."

My friend Asya, who is Jewish, thought otherwise when I brought up the issue on the phone the next day. "If there were statues of famous Nazis around, even ones with replaced heads and nameplates, I still wouldn't want to pass them every day," she said. "I mean, ugh, what a slap in the face!"

I see her point. To those upset about the monuments that were recently toppled, I guess I'd say, "Look, times change. Jefferson Davis overlooked your godforsaken traffic circle for one hundred years. Now we'll just put him in storage and make it someone else's turn for a while."

"Who could argue with that?" I asked my friends John and Lynette, who have a house not far from the Sea Section. I'd thought the streets in our neighborhood were named after the developer's children, but it seems I was wrong. "That's Lee Avenue as in *Robert E.*," John said. "Stuart Avenue as in *Jeb*, and Jackson as in *Stonewall*."

When I repeated this to Amy, she said, "What about Scotch Bonnet Drive?"

"That's after, um, General Jedediah Scotch Bonnet," I told her.

Then there was the street called Coon Crossing. A year earlier I might have thought nothing of it, but everything was getting a second look now. I was surprised to learn that John and Lynette's neighborhood in Raleigh—Cameron Village—was now called simply the Village District, this because the *Cameron* it was named after had been a plantation owner. This made me wonder about the men behind my elementary and high schools. Who was E. C. Brooks? Jesse Sanderson?

In the meantime, Uncle Ben's rice was now called Ben's Original. The box was still orange, but there was no longer a face on it. Eskimo Pies disappeared as well.

"I was fine with all this Black Lives Matter stuff until they went after both Aunt Jemima *and* Mrs. Butterworth's," our friend Bermey said. "Now, I'm like, 'Hey, don't fuck with my syrup!'"

One of the many shops on the island that sells inflatable rafts and inexpensive clothing had a Confederate flag beach towel in its window. I saw a fair number of these in eastern North Carolina. Some were discreet—a decal on a windshield—and others were loud: full-sized standards billowing in front of houses, often beside a TRUMP flag or affixed to massive pickup trucks that would tear up and down the main road. The trucks were unnaturally high off the ground and most often had jacked-up front wheels that made them look like they were forever going uphill—Carolina Squats, they were called, or bro dozers. Their mufflers had been modified as well, or perhaps they'd been removed altogether. Engines roared as if to say, "Asshole coming through!" Should there be any doubt that the driver was insecure regarding his masculinity, one could often find a pair of lemon-sized testicles dangling from the trailer hitch.

"Lord, son," Bermey said when, astonished, I described them to him. "You ain't never seen *Truck Nutz?*"

I was eight when we moved south from New York. It was the first time I heard the words *Yankee* and *Rebel.* In school, at Cub Scouts and the country club, you were on either one side or the other. People who win the war move on. People who lose turn their flags into beach towels and hang hard rubber testicles from their bumpers. They make it easy for the rest of us to hide. "Over there!" we say, pointing to a bro dozer with a Confederate flag affixed to it. "*That's* what a racist looks like."

When I was in seventh grade, I acted as campaign manager for Dwight Bunch, one of the three Black students at Carroll Junior High. He ran for class president—and won—with my brilliant slogan "We Like Dwight a Bunch." Two years later our school was desegregated. Fights broke out in the parking lot. My friend Ted had his nose broken with a Coke bottle. In our twenties we both dated a number of Black guys, which I always thought made us the opposite of racists. I didn't have sex with them because of their color but just because they were there and willing. Now I was reading that sleeping with Black guys *meant* you were racist, that you were exoticizing them.

Everything was suspect, and everywhere you turned there was an article titled "_____'s Race Problem."

It could be about anyone: an actor who'd never had a costar of color, a comedian who used the word *Negro* twenty years ago. The articles were always written by white people in their early twenties.

I saw the phrase *POC (White Passing)* in the signature of an email someone sent and wondered how long that had been a thing.

Reckoning was the word I kept hearing. It was time for a racial reckoning.

We stayed at the beach for two weeks and returned to New York just as the protests had petered out into bike-riding opportunities. Flash mobs of predominantly white people would pedal up the avenues, three thousand strong, blocking traffic, chanting, "Whose streets? Our streets!" and, occasionally, "Black Lives Matter!"—but strangely, in the singsongy way a fishmonger might call, "Fresh-caught haddock!"

I came upon a bike march one Saturday afternoon, the last day of spring, at around five o'clock. People lined Third Avenue, most raising their phones to shoot pictures and videos, or to turn their backs on the cyclists and take selfies. Beside me stood two white girls in their early twenties, both frantically texting. Both had tans. "Where can *we* get bikes?" one asked the other. She tugged down her mask and commenced filming herself. "Black Lives Matter!" she shouted. "Wooooo!"

"How do I get across?" asked a frail-looking elderly woman who had suddenly appeared beside me. Her rust-colored wig was pulled down low on her forehead, and she wore a sun visor. In her hand was a heavy-looking bag from the nearby drugstore.

"You wait until these people are *done,*" snapped one of the suntanned girls.

I—who, of course, needed to pee—was wondering the same thing: *How might I cross? How do I, how do all of us, get to the other side?*

Happy-Go-Lucky

Something about a car running over a policeman and a second officer being injured. This is my assessment of a news story broadcast on the television in my father's room at Springmoor, where he's been living for the past three years. It is early April, three days before his ninety-eighth birthday, and Amy, Hugh, and I have just flown to Raleigh from New York. The plan is to hang out for a while and then drive to our house on Emerald Isle.

Dad is in his wheelchair, dressed and groomed for our visit. Hair combed. Real shoes on his feet. A red bandanna tied around his neck. "Well, hey!" he calls as we walk in, an old turtle raising his head toward the sun. "Gosh, it's good to see you kids!"

As Amy and I move in to embrace him, Hugh wonders if we could possibly turn off the TV.

"Well, sure," my father, still smothered in grown children, says. "I don't even know why it's on, to tell you the truth."

Hugh takes the remote off the bedside table, and after he's killed the television, Amy asks if he can figure out the radio. As a non–blood relative, that seems to be his role during our visits to Springmoor—the servant.

"Find us a jazz station," I tell him.

"There we go!" my father says. "That would be fantastic!"

Neither Amy nor I care about the news anymore, at least the political news. I am vaguely aware that Andrew Cuomo has fallen out of favor, and that people who aren't me will be receiving government checks for some reason or other, but that's about it. When Trump was president I started every morning by reading the *New York Times,* followed by the *Washington Post,* and would track both papers' websites regularly throughout the day. To be less than vigilant was to fall behind, and was there anything worse than not knowing what Stephen Miller just said about Wisconsin? My friend Mike likened this constant monitoring to having a second job. It was exhausting, and the moment that Biden was sworn in to office I let it all go. When the new president speaks, I feel the way I do on a plane when the pilot announces that after reaching our cruising altitude he will head due north, or take a left at Lake Erie. *You don't need to tell me about your job,* I always think. *Just, you know, do it.*

It's so freeing, no longer listening to political podcasts—no longer being enraged. I still browse the dailies, skipping over the stories about COVID, as I am finished with all that as well.

The moment I got my first shot of the vaccine, I started thinking of the coronavirus the way I think of scurvy—something from a long-ago time that can no longer hurt me, something that mainly pirates get. "Yes," the papers would say, "but what if there's a powerful surge this summer? This Christmas? A year from now? What if our next pandemic is worse than this one? What if it kills all the fish and cattle and poultry and affects our skin's reaction to sunlight? What if it forces everyone to live underground and subsist on earthworms?"

My father tested positive for the coronavirus shortly before Christmas, at around the time he started wheeling himself to the front desk at Springmoor and asking if anyone there had seen his mother. He hasn't got Alzheimer's, nothing that severe. Rather, he's what used to be called "soft in the head." Gaga. It's a relatively new development—aside from the time he was discovered on the floor of his house, dehydrated and suffering from a bladder infection, he's always been not just lucid but commanding.

"If it happens several times in one day, someone on the staff will contact me," Lisa told us over the phone. "Then I'll call and say, 'Dad, your mother died in 1976 and is buried beside your father at the Rural Cemetery in Cortland, New York. You bought the plot next to theirs, so that's where you'll be going.'"

There had to be a gentler way to say this, but I'm not sure the news really registered, especially after his diagnosis, when he was at his weakest. Every time the phone rang I expected to hear that he had died. But my father recovered. "*Without* being hospitalized," I told my cousin Nancy. "*Plus,* he lost ten pounds!" Not that he needed to.

When I ask him what it was like to have the coronavirus, he offers a false-sounding laugh. He does that a lot now—"Ha ha!" I suspect it is a cover for his failed hearing, that rather than saying, "Could you repeat that?," he figures it's a safe bet you are delivering a joke of some sort. "Hugh and I just went to Louisville to see his mother," I'd said to my dad the last time we were at Springmoor. "Joan is ninety now and has blood cancer."

"Ha ha!"

That was on Halloween. Socially distanced visits were allowed in the outdoor courtyard of my father's building, and after our allotted thirty minutes were up, an aide disguised as a witch wheeled him back to his room.

"The costumes must do a real number on some of the residents," Amy said as we walked with Hugh to our rental car. " 'And then a vampire came to take my blood pressure!'

" 'Sure he did, Grandpa.' "

A few days after we saw him, all visits were canceled, and Springmoor was locked down. No one in or out except staff, and all the residents confined to their rooms. The policy wasn't reversed until six months later. That's when we flew down from New York to see him.

"You look great, Dad," Amy says in a voice that is almost but not quite a shout. Hugh has finally found a jazz station and managed to tune out the static.

"Well, I'm a hundred years old!" my father tells us. "Can you beat that?"

"Ninety-eight," Amy corrects him. "And not quite yet. Your birthday is on Monday and today is only Friday."

"A hundred years old!"

This isn't soft-headedness but a lifelong tendency to exaggerate. "What the hell are you still doing up?" he'd demand of my brother, my sisters, and me every school night of our lives. "It's one o'clock in the morning!"

We'd point to the nearest clock. "Actually it's nine forty-five."

"It's one o'clock, dammit!"

"Then how come *Barnaby Jones* is still on?"

"Go to bed!"

Amy has brought my father some chocolate turtles and, as he looks on, she opens the box and hands him one. "Your room looks good too. It's clean, and your stuff fits in real well."

"It's not bad, is it?" my father says. "You might not believe it, but this is the exact same square footage as the house—the basement of it, anyway."

This is simply not true, but we let it go.

"There are a few things I'd like to get rid of, but as a whole it's not too cluttered," he observes, turning a jerky semicircle in his wheelchair. "That was a real problem for me once upon a time. I used to be *the king* of clutter."

Were I his decorator I'd definitely lose the Christmas tree that stands collecting dust on the console beneath his TV. It is a foot and a half tall and made of plastic. Naked, it might be OK, but its baubles—which are the size of juniper berries and gaudy—depress me. Beside it is a stack of cards sent by people I don't know, or whose names I only vaguely recognize from the Greek Orthodox Church. "Has the priest been by?" I ask.

My father nods. "A few times. He doesn't much like me, though."

Amy takes a seat on the bed. "Why not?"

He laughs. "Let's just say I'm not as generous as I could be!"

My father is thinner than the last time I saw him, but somehow his face is fuller. Something else is different as well, but I can't put my finger on it. It's like when celebrities get work done. I can see they've undergone a change, but I can never tell exactly what it is. *The eyes? The mouth?* I'll wonder, examining a photo on some gossip site. "You don't look the same for some reason," I say to my father.

He turns from me to Hugh, and then to Amy. "Well, *you* do. All of you do. The only one who's changed is me. I'm a hundred years old!"

"Ninety-eight on Monday," Amy says.

"A hundred years old!"

"Have you had your COVID vaccine?" I ask, knowing that he has.

"I'm not sure," he says. "Maybe."

I pick up a salmon carved out of something hard and porous, an antler, maybe. It used to be in his basement office at the house. This was before he turned every room into an office and buried himself in envelopes. "Hugh and me and Amy, we've each had one shot."

My father laughs. "Well, good for you. I haven't had a drink since I got here."

At first I take this as a non sequitur, then I realize that by *shot* he thinks we mean a shot of alcohol.

"They don't let you drink?" I ask.

"Oh, you can have a little, I guess, but it's not easy. You have to order it in advance, like medicine, and you only get a thimbleful," he says in his whisper of a voice.

"What do you think would happen if you had a screwdriver?" Amy asks.

He thinks for a moment. "I'd probably get an erection!"

I really like this new version of my father. He's charming and positive and full of surprises. "One of the things I like about us as a family is that we laugh," he says. "Always! As far back as I can remember. It's what we're known for!"

Most of that laughter had been directed at him, and erupted the moment he left whichever room the rest of us were occupying. A Merriment Club member he definitely was not. But I like that he remembers things differently. "My offbeat sense of humor has won me a lot of friends," he tells us. "A hell of a lot."

"Friends *here*?" Amy asks.

"All over the damn place! Even the kids I used to roller-skate with—they come by sometimes."

He opens his hand and we see that the chocolate turtle he's been holding has melted. Amy fetches some toilet paper from the bathroom, and he sits passively as she cleans him off. "What is it you're wearing?" he asks.

She takes a step back so that he can see her black-and-white polka-dot shift. Over it is a Japanese denim shirt with coaster-sized smiley-face patches running up and down the sleeves. Her friend Paul recently told her that she dresses like a fat person, the defiant sort who thinks, *You want to laugh? I'll give you something to laugh at.*

"Interesting," my father says.

Whenever the conversation stalls, he turns it back to one of several subjects, the first being the inexpensive guitar he bought me when I was a child and insisted on bringing with him to Springmoor—this after it had sat neglected in a closet for more than half a century. "I'm trying to teach myself to play, but I just can't find the time to practice."

It seems to me that all he has is time. What else is there to do here, shut up in his room? "I've got to make some music!" he says. As he shakes his fist in frustration, I notice that he still has some chocolate beneath his fingernails.

"You're too hard on yourself, Dad," Amy tells him. "You don't have to do everything, you know. Maybe it's OK to just relax for a change."

His second go-to topic is the artwork hanging on his walls, most of it bought by him and my mother in the seventies and early eighties. "Now this," he says, pointing to a framed seri-graph over his bed, "this I could look at every minute of the day." It is a sentimental, naïf-style street scene of Paris in the early twentieth century—a veritable checklist of tropes and clichés by Michel Delacroix, who defines himself as a "painter of dreams and of the poetic past." On the two occasions when my father visited me in the actual Paris, he couldn't leave fast enough. It's only in pictures that he can stand the place. "I've got to write this guy a letter and tell him what his work means to me," he says. "The trick is finding the damn time!"

Two of the paintings in the room are by my father, done in the late sixties. His art phase came from nowhere, and during its brief six-month span he was prolific, churning out twenty or so canvases, most done with a palette knife rather than a brush. All of them are copies—of van Gogh, of Zurbarán and Picasso. They wouldn't fool anyone, but as children we were awed by his talent. The problem was what to paint, or, in his case, to copy. Some of his choices were questionable—a stage-coach silhouetted against a tangerine-colored sunset comes to mind—but in retrospect it fit right in with the rest of the house. Back in the seventies we thought of our color scheme as permanently modern. What would dare replace all that orange and brown and avocado? By the early eighties it was laughable, but now it's back and we're able to think fondly of our milk-chocolate walls and the stout wicker burro that used to pout atop the piano, one of our father's acrylic bullfighters seemingly afire on the wall behind it.

When Dad retired from IBM, the artwork became a greater part of his identity. He *had been* an engineer, but he *was* an art lover. This didn't extend to museums—who needed them when he had his living room! "I'm an actual collector, while David, he's more of an investor," he sniffed to my friend Lee after I bought a Picasso that was painted by Picasso and did not look—dare I say it—like cake frosting.

Then there's my father's collection of masks, some of which are hanging high on the wall over his bed. The best of them were made by tribes in the Pacific Northwest and Alaska, bought on fly-fishing trips. A few others are African or Mexican. They used to leer down from the paneled wall above the staircase in our house, and it is odd but not unpleasant to see them in this new setting. When walking down the hall at Springmoor, I always peek into the other rooms, none of which resemble my father's. There are the neighbors, and then there is Dad—Dad, who is listening to Eric Dolphy and holding the guitar he has never in his life played. "You know, four of the strings on this thing came off my old violin, the one I had in grade school!"

No, they didn't, but who cares? Before his mind started failing, my father consumed a steady diet of Fox News and conservative talk radio that kept him at a constant boiling point. "Who's that Black guy?" he demanded in 2014. The family was together at the Sea Section, and we were talking about Michael Brown, who'd been shot and killed three months earlier in Ferguson, Missouri.

"What Black guy?" I asked.

"Oh, you know the one."

"Bill Cosby?" Amy offered.

"Gil Scott-Heron?" I asked.

"Stevie Wonder?" Gretchen called from the living room.

Lisa said, "Denzel Washington?"

"You know who I mean," Dad said. "He's got that son."

"Jesse Jackson?"

"He's the one. Always stirring up trouble."

Now, though, our father has taken a few steps back and, like me, seems all the better for it. "How did you feel when Biden was elected?" I ask. The question is a violation of the pact Amy and I made before arriving: Don't rile him up, don't confuse him.

"Actually," he says, "I was for that other one."

Hugh says, "Trump."

My father nods. "That's right. I believed what he was telling us. And, well, it seems that I was wrong. That guy was bad news."

Never did I expect to hear this: Trump was "bad" *and* "I was wrong"—practically in the same breath. "Who are you?" I want to ask the gentle gnome in front of me, "and what have you done with Lou Sedaris?"

"So, Biden...I guess he's OK," my father says, looking, with his red bandanna, like the leftist he never was.

Amy, Hugh, and I are just recovering when an aide walks in and announces that it is five o'clock, time for dinner. "I'll wheel Mr. Sedaris down..."

"Oh, we'll take him," Amy says.

"Take what?" my father asks, confused by the sudden activity.

I push him out the door and past a TV upon which the news is playing. Again, the incident at the Capitol. Some people hit by a car, someone shot.

"This is like that old joke," I say to my father as we near the dining room. "A man bitches to his wife, 'You're always

189

pushing me around and talking behind my back.' And she says, 'What do you expect—you're in a wheelchair!' "

My father roars, "Ha!"

The dining room, which fits maybe six tables, is full when we arrive. Women greatly outnumber men, and no one except for us and the staff is ambulatory. The air should smell like food, but instead it smells like Amy, her perfume. She wears so much that it manages to both precede her *and* trail behind her, lingering long after she's moved on. That said, I like it. A combination of five different scents, none of which is flowery or particularly sweet, it leaves her smelling like a strange cookie, maybe one with pencil shavings in it.

"Eat, why don't you?" my father says.

I am conscious of everyone watching. *Visitors! Lou has visitors!*

While Amy and Hugh talk to an aide, my father looks up and pats the space beside him at the table. "Stay for dinner. They can make you anything you want."

I can't remember my mother's last words to me. They were delivered over the phone at the end of a casual conversation. "See you," she might have said, or "I'll call back in a few days."

And in the thoughtless way you respond when you think you have forever with the person on the other end of the line, I likely said, "OK."

My father's last words to me, spoken in the too-hot, too-bright dining room at his assisted living facility three days before his ninety-eighth birthday, are "Don't go yet. Don't leave."

My last words to him—and I think they are as telling as his, given all we've been through—are "We need to get to the beach before the grocery stores close." They look cold on paper, and when he dies a few weeks later and I *realize* they are the last words I said to him, I will think, *Maybe I can warm them up onstage when I read this part out loud.* For, rather than thinking of his death, I will be thinking of the story of his death, so much so that after his funeral Amy will ask, "Did I see you taking notes during the service?"

There'll be no surprise in her voice. Rather, it will be the way you might playfully scold a squirrel: "Did you just jump up from the deck and completely empty that bird feeder?"

The squirrel and me—it's in our nature, though maybe not forever. For our natures, I have just recently learned from my father, can change. Or maybe they're simply revealed, and the dear, cheerful man I saw that afternoon at Springmoor was there all along, smothered in layers of rage and impatience that burned away as he blazed into the homestretch.

For the moment, though, leaving the dining room in the company of Hugh and Amy, I am thinking that we'll have to do this again, and soon. Fly to Raleigh. See Dad. Maybe have a picnic in his room. I'll talk Gretchen into coming. Lisa will be there too, and our brother, Paul. All of us together and laughing so loudly we'll be asked by some aide to close the door. Because really, isn't that what we're known for?

A Better Place

Doesn't all our greatest art address the subject of death—its cruelty, its inevitability? The shadow it casts on our all-too-brief lives? "What does it all mean?" we ask ourselves.

Allow me to tell you: Death means that the dinner reservation you made for a party of seven needs to be upped to ten, then lowered to nine and then upped again, this time to fourteen. Eighteen will ultimately show up, so you will have to sit at a four-top on the other side of the room with people you just vaguely remember, listening as the fun table, the one with your sparkling sister at it, laughs and laughs. You, meanwhile, have to hear things like "Well, I know that your father did his best."

People love saying this when a parent dies. It's the first thing they reach for. A man can beat his wife with car antennas, can trade his children for drugs or motorcycles, but still, when he finally, mercifully, dies, his survivors will have to hear from some know-nothing at the post-funeral dinner that he did his best. This, I'm guessing, is based on the premise that we *all* give 110 percent *all* the time, regarding *everything:* our careers, our relationships, the attention we pay to our appearance, etc.

"Look around," I want to say. "Very few people are actually doing the best they can. That's why they get fired from their jobs. That's why they get arrested and divorced. It's why their teeth fall out. Do you think the 'chef' responsible for this waterlogged spanakopita is giving it *his* all? Is sitting across from me, spouting clichés and platitudes, honestly the best *you* can do?"

Also, don't use the word *passed* at this table unless it's as in, "Tula passed me the salt so I could flavor my tasteless tzatziki sauce," or "I knew we were driving too slowly on our way to the funeral when the hearse passed us and the man driving it gave me the finger."

My father did not *pass*. Neither did he *depart*. He died.

Why the euphemisms? Who are they helping? I remember hearing a woman on the radio a few years back reflecting on where she was the moment that Prince, the musician, "transitioned."

Really? I thought. *And when exactly did he become a woman? Days before his fatal drug overdose?*

Also, can we give the whole *looking down from heaven* bit a rest? This, as in, "I'm sure your mother is looking down right now at you and your family..."

Sure about that, are you? Sure there's a heaven right above the cloud cover, one that no satellite or spacecraft has ever picked up, and that my long-dead mother can peer down from it and spot my brother, my sisters, and me *indoors, some of us with hats on,* out of the roughly eight billion other people on earth, and without her glasses, because they weren't with her in the box she was burned to ashes in? Because if that were possible, she wouldn't be thinking, *I'm so proud of my son,* but *What's he listening to* that *asshole for?*

As for my father, if anything, he's looking *up* at me, not down. He was ninety-eight—"A blessing," you keep saying. "He must have been a wonderful man to have been rewarded with such a long life." As if it worked that way, and extra years were tacked on for good behavior. Any number of decent people die young. You know who's living a "good long life"? Dick Cheney. Henry Kissinger. Rupert Murdoch.

"He'll always be with you" is another tiresome chestnut I'd be happy never to hear again. In response to it, I say, "What if I don't *want* him with me?" What if sixty-four years of constant criticism and belittlement were enough, and I'm actually fine with my father and me going our separate ways, him in a cooler at the funeral home and me here at the kids' table? He won't be in his grave for another few days. Is that the "better place" you've been assuring me he's headed to—the cemetery we pass on our way to the airport? The plot with a view of the Roy Rogers parking lot? And what exactly is it better than? This restaurant, clearly, but what else? This state? This country? This earth?

No offense, but how can you be so sure of his whereabouts? You didn't even know where the men's room was until I told you, so why should I suddenly believe that you're omniscient? The best you can say with any degree of certainty is that my father's in *another* place, meaning *not* the only restaurant in town that could accommodate a party of eighteen with five hours' notice, which, hint, it could do only because nobody else wants to eat here, especially me—it's just that I need to keep my strength up. Because I'm grieving.

Lady Marmalade

One night when I was young—maybe ten years old, or eleven—I complained at the dinner table that my stomach was bothering me. It hadn't stopped me from cleaning my plate, so I likely mentioned it in an effort to get out of school the following day. My plan was to invent a symptom at six, add a headache at bedtime, and maybe toss in some reported diarrhea in the morning. I just needed a short break from the fifth grade, I guess.

"Let's see how you feel later on," my mother said. "Maybe there's something going around."

I was at my desk not long afterward, brushing out my guinea pig, when my father popped in. It was always weird having him in my room, so I stood up, hoping it would make him leave faster. "Stomach still bothering you?" he asked.

I said in a weak voice that it was, though he wasn't the one who could keep me out of school the next day. That sort of thing was my mother's duty, not his.

"It could be hemorrhoids," he said. "Ever think of that?"

As an adult, looking back, I'm like, *What kind of kid gets hemorrhoids? And what would they have to do with his stomach?* At the time, though, I had no idea what he was talking about.

"Come into the bathroom," he said. "The one upstairs, not the one down here."

I put my guinea pig back into her pen and followed my father upstairs. In the bathroom he closed and locked the door. Then he told me to pull my shorts and underwear down and to lean over the counter that the sink was in. My dad spent a lot of time in his underpants. He was in them now, as a matter of fact. They were briefs, not boxers, worn most evenings with a white or blue button-down work shirt. His tie was loosened and hung around his neck like a noose.

Aside from him charging around the house with only half his clothes on, we were a pretty modest group. It made me uncomfortable, Dad seeing my butt, but I did what he told me to. I'm guessing he chose the upstairs bathroom because of its layout. It was designed in such a way that I could bend forward with my head in the sink and he could sit on the toilet, lid down, with a prime, brightly lit view of, well, my asshole. "Spread your legs," he said. "Wider." He didn't insert anything. Rather, he just gazed at it, like it was a gem or something.

"All right," he said after a while. "You can pull your pants back up."

In my memory, this happened at least two more times during my youth: stomachache, call to the bathroom, anal exam.

When I mentioned it to Hugh years later, he said, "Did you tell anyone?"

"Of course not," I said. "I mean, it was embarrassing."

When I was fourteen, I awoke one morning to find blood in my underwear. It freaked me out. *Where had it come from, and why?* I wondered.

Normally I'd have gone to Mom about it. Worried, though, that she would tell my father and that he'd have me bend over the sink again, I took my underpants and buried them under some leaves in the deep ravine beside our house. All kinds of things were buried there over the years, and not just by me.

My father was strange in a lot of ways. When my sister Lisa, who was the oldest, got her first bra, he called her to his spot at the head of the table. Then he stood up and—again, in his underpants—slowly undid the buttons on her blouse.

"Ha ha," we all said. "Lisa wears a bra now!"

"Oh, Lou," my mother scolded.

When Gretchen and I were in high school, our parents took us to New Orleans for a weekend. I'm guessing it was my mother's idea and that we went on her dime, as we stayed in a nice hotel and had breakfast at Brennan's, which was a big deal. The whole trip was a big deal, and not a moment of it was wasted on my sister or me. "Lady Marmalade" by Labelle had just come out and seemed to be playing everywhere. It was set in New Orleans, so it felt to us that, being there, we had an inside scoop on the song, the way you would if you'd been in, say, Ventura, California, when "Ventura Highway" was released by the band America two years earlier.

My dad and I were on Bourbon Street, waiting for Gretchen and my mother, who had ducked into a souvenir shop. "Lady Marmalade" was drifting out of a bar, and as they emerged and walked toward us, he said of my sister, who was tottering on platform shoes, a straw hat on her head, looking, I'd later realize, a lot like Jodie Foster in *Taxi Driver,* "God, she's got a great set of pins!"

I didn't know what pins were, and when I later learned that they were legs, I thought, *Well, that's a nice thing to say about someone.* In general, I mean. If that person isn't, you know, your daughter. His voice in that moment had been different, wolfish, and the first word of his sentence—*God*—suggested regret. Like too bad Gretchen was related to him and he couldn't pursue her. It was an odd little moment, but I chalked it up to being out of town, to New Orleans and *"Voulez-vous coucher avec moi?,"* which our waiter at Galatoire's that evening translated to *"Would you like to have some fun with me?"*

Back in Raleigh a few months later, Dad asked Lisa, who was seventeen, if she would go with him into the woods behind our house and pose topless. "I want to take a few pictures," he told her. "It's art photography, not smut. I have a magazine I can show you. I mean, this is strictly professional."

I'd seen the magazine he was referring to. We all had. *Popular Photography*, it was called. He started subscribing after he got the fancy Nikon camera he hardly ever used. Most of the articles were technical: how to light beef, what exposures to use at dusk. There were usually photos of nature in it—an eerie close-up of a bee or a termite; a colorful male hummingbird stabbing a daylily, his wings a frenzied cape—that kind of thing. There were bold landscapes and portraits. Then there was the sort of art photos Dad was referring to: nudes, always of young women. The difference between these pictures and the ones I'd scowl at in the *Playboy*s he kept hidden in his closet was that, in the former, the subject's eyes—if not closed—gazed dreamily beyond you, to the far distance, where hope and freedom lay. In *Playboy*, on the other hand, the young women engaged you. *Like what you see?* they seemed to say. *I like you too!* Often their fingers were in their mouths.

Lisa understood the kind of photos my father meant. Posing topless in the forest for him would not involve the "Look into the camera!" and "Smile, dammit!" that he barked as he snapped our annual Christmas pictures, but still she said no way.

"But you're beautiful!"

"Yeah, right," she said.

Scorned, he told her not to get too stuck-up about it. "All you've really got is your long hair."

A few years later he walked in on Gretchen and her boyfriend having sex in her bedroom, which was in the basement, beside mine. At the sound of the door opening, Jeff rolled off the mattress and onto the floor—out of sight, or so he thought. "Stand up," my father commanded.

From then on, Dad never looked at Gretchen the same way. Not long afterward, she went to the mall and had her picture taken at one of those studios that embossed its signature in the lower right-hand corner of the print, like it was a work of art. Olan Mills, I think the place was called. Everyone loved the photo except our dad, who held it in his hands for a moment and then tossed it down, saying, "You look like a tired old whore."

There were umpteen other things our father did and said over the years. It wasn't that he violated our bodies. He just wanted us to know that they were as much his as ours. The comments he made—we just brushed them off or else laughed at him. "If only I were thirty-five years younger," he'd moan on the beach at the sight of Amy in a bikini.

"That guy," we'd say. "What a creep!"

After we all left home, he bought a number of apartments near the university. The tenants were students, and he'd regularly drop in on them, supposedly to collect rent or to do some minor repair. "So I'm down on Clark Avenue to fix the hot water heater," he'd say, drink in his hand at the end of the day, "and I walk into the upstairs bedroom to catch Cal Compton having sex with his girlfriend! Can you believe it?"

"Did you knock first?" we'd ask.

"What do I have to knock for? I own the place!"

He always acted so surprised. "So what do I find but Brenda Cash stepping out of her bathroom stark naked at, get this, three in the afternoon!" As if that were the story—that she didn't shower on his schedule.

We looked at all of this differently after our sister Tiffany accused our father of sexually abusing her. Our mother was long dead by this time. Tiffany was around forty and unemployed. When asked why she hadn't brought this up sooner, she said that it had been buried in her subconscious. It might have remained there, like a pharaoh's tomb, had her therapist not helped her unearth it.

"What exactly did Dad do?" we asked.

She said that she couldn't remember, but that didn't mean it didn't happen—in fact it was just the opposite. "It was obviously so awful that my mind shut down."

"OK," we said, dubious. It wasn't like Lisa or Gretchen or Amy saying such a thing. Tiffany wasn't trustworthy the way they were. She wasn't sound.

As the years passed, her story changed slightly. Suddenly she remembered Dad entering her room in the middle of the night.

"He did that all the time," I reminded her. "Nothing drives him crazier than a window being open and the heat or air-conditioning leaking out. You know how mental he gets over his electric bill."

Amy shared a room with Tiffany, and she couldn't recall our father ever coming in after they were in bed. This is what happens in a family when these kinds of charges are leveled against someone. You think, *Well, that couldn't have taken place* here. *Not in this house, the one where I had my ass-hole stared at, the one where Lisa was invited to pose topless.* "Sure, Dad can be creepy," the rest of us said, "but abuse? That's going too far!"

"If he was going to have sex with someone, wouldn't it be Amy?" we asked one another. "No offense, but, I mean, she *is* prettier and a lot easier to handle."

Amy was always strong, though, as were Gretchen and, to a lesser extent, Lisa. Tiffany was the fragile one.

In the wake of #MeToo I know how brutal this sounds, but it was hard to believe much of what our sister said. By this time, we all thought of Tiffany as crazy. She was living just outside Boston then, and her life made very little sense to us. Things that mattered to me and the rest of my family—stability, love, having a beautiful home—were not just unimportant to her but worthy of contempt. I know that she took drugs—we all did at one point or another, some of us massively—but the rest of us managed to hold down jobs. We didn't go through one another's medicine cabinets and swallow whatever we found, right there on the spot.

This is not to put her down. If anything, it fortified her argument. For wasn't this what sexually abused people *did*? All she was missing was specifics.

I know that Tiffany had sex for money. "There's a guy who's paying me to fuck him with a strap-on dildo," she said to me on the phone one afternoon, laughing. I was in Normandy and she'd called collect. "Now he wants to do it to *me,* so I'm wondering, have you ever used Anbesol to numb the pain in your asshole?"

One thing you never want is for your youngest sister to call for advice on anal sex, especially when she's getting paid for it. I don't know why that last bit makes it worse, but it does somehow.

"You are talking to the wrong person," I told her.

She thought for a moment. "Then put Hugh on the phone."

"He's the wrong person as well," I said. "You need to call...another house."

Something in Tiffany's early life seemed to have kicked her forward, past the dating and puppy-love periods the rest of us went through. There was a phase missing. Anyone could see that. This too made us wonder if something had happened. Ask for details—"What exactly did Dad do?"—and she'd say, every time, "I never said he threw me against a '57 Chevy and fucked me."

"Well, then..."

"That's not what I said, that he threw me against a Chevy and fucked me."

"Great. Now that that's cleared up, I'm just wondering..."

"He didn't fuck me against a Chevy."

"Then what exactly...?"

"I never said anything about him fucking me."

My dad did have a '57 Chevy, but Tiffany was only two years old when he got rid of it and bought a red '64 Mustang.

What our sister came to call "physical abuse," the rest of

us just thought of as punishment—not fun, certainly, but far from exceptional, at least in that era. It wasn't uncommon for my mother to slap one of us across the face. She didn't go wild, but maybe once a year the cobra would strike, and, hand on your red-hot cheek, you'd find yourself saying, incredulously, as if you might be wrong about this, "Did you just slap me across the face?"

My father once clamped his hands around my neck, lifted me off the ground, and pinned me to the wall. My feet were off the floor, and until the laundry room was painted fifty-five years later, you could still see the smudges my shoes had made as I struggled in vain for purchase. He would hit me with paddles. He shoved me into trees and whacked me over the head with heavy serving spoons, but I still wouldn't say that he abused me, maybe because, if I ever have children myself—which is unlikely—I reserve the right to similarly rough them up should the situation call for it. "Damned kids, going through my pockets and taking all my change," I'll thunder. "I reached in for a quarter at the grocery store today and pulled out nothing but a paper clip!"

I always dreamed of saying to my father in such moments, "Keep your pants on for ten goddamn minutes and maybe we wouldn't paw through them for money."

I don't know why some people can look back at such things and laugh while others can't. Tiffany wanted a reason why her life was such a mess, one that didn't involve the depression and mental illness that have plagued both sides of our family for generations and will unjustly infect one person but not the next. As the years passed and parenting became a verb, behavior that was once normal enough—calling your child a loser, whipping them with a belt or a switch—was seen in a different light. We who were beaten and belittled often reflect upon it with something akin to pride. It speaks to our resilience and our ability to forgive. Not Tiffany, though. To her it was criminal.

"So I see this woman hitting her daughter on the street the other day, and do you think I called the cops?" she asked me on the phone one night. "Fuck, no! Instead I went up to her and said, 'Hey, why don't you let me watch your fucking kid for a while?' And you know, David, if everybody did that, people wouldn't have to grow up the way we did."

She could be very grandiose, Tiffany, very stand-back-while-I-save-the-world. That said, who's going to turn her daughter over to a complete stranger, one who just put the word *fucking* before *kid*?

After Tiffany and I stopped talking in 2004, she started telling people that *I* had abused her and that she had always been afraid of me.

"Really?" I said when Lisa told me.

I remember sticking pins in Tiffany's ass when she was sitting in the butterfly chair—the prime spot in front of the basement TV—and I wanted to get her out of it. But it's not like I did it every day, and I was, like, ten at the time. I remember riding her about her buckteeth, calling her a beaver, and so forth, but, again, we were kids.

Tiffany was twelve when I left for college, and a few years

later she ran away from home. The police brought her back, and she took off again a week later. This landed her in Élan, a behavior modification center in Maine that called itself a school, though the students/inmates were in class for only one hour per day. The rest of their time was spent causing one another irreparable damage. It's shocking the number of alumni—my sister included—who went on to take their own lives.

After two years of torture, she returned to Raleigh and enrolled in high school, not the one the rest of us had attended but a different one where she wouldn't know anybody. Her grades were mainly Fs, and I'm not sure that she even graduated. I remember her spending nights at my apartment, usually after some fight with our parents. Like me, she never learned to drive, so some guy or other would bring her over.

Tiffany was a dynamic person. Her voice was husky. She laughed easily and could talk to anyone. This made her a hit at the fancy food store she started working at after school. She'd been there for all of six months before a customer recruited her to work for Neuhaus Chocolates. Tiffany moved to New York and was there for three years. She stayed in Harlem. She stayed in Midtown with some Jewish girl she said was crazy. She stayed with a coke dealer in Queens. One evening at a nightclub she was rushed to the hospital and learned there was a baby the size of a troll doll living in one of her fallopian tubes. An operation was performed. My parents flew up, and my father asked, "So, was it a boy or a girl?"

"Oh, Lou," my mother scolded.

I liked that when the doctor walked in and asked Tiffany if she had any questions regarding her recovery, she answered, weakly, in front of Mom and Dad, "Yes. When can I have sex again?"

She could be terribly funny like that. During the chocolate years I remember her visiting me in Chicago, and us getting high and laughing. Us on pot and ecstasy and acid and coke, me thinking that maybe things were looking up for her, that she could leave the horrible reform school behind.

Toward the end of her life—the last few years of it—she'd phone our father and threaten to go public with her abuse story. "And the thing is that she calls *collect,*" Amy told me. "And he accepts the charges!"

Whenever Dad asked Tiffany for specifics, she'd say, just as she'd said to us, "I never said you fucked me against a '57 Chevy. That's not what I'm saying."

She just remembered him coming into her room.

"And how old were you at the time?" he'd ask.

She couldn't recall.

"Four? Six? Ten?"

No answer.

"Christ almighty, that girl," he'd say.

Once, with the help of a friend, she phoned our father and taped the conversation, hoping he would incriminate himself and she could sue him for ruining her life. "Do you think I'm sexy?" was one of the questions she asked him.

It was so trashy. "I was going to give the money to charity," she insisted when asked about it afterward. "I wasn't going to keep it for myself."

Another time she flew home and threw a hibachi at him. "Was it the one in the carport?" our sister Gretchen asked. "Did she break it? I wanted that hibachi!"

By then our father was supporting Tiffany, though barely, giving her just enough to scrape by. At the time of her second suicide attempt—the successful one—she was living in a group home with two men, both of whom had long fingernails and neither of whom noticed the smell of her decomposing body. Five days she was there, in a hot, un-air-conditioned room. "Well, we're heavy smokers," they explained when asked about it.

On the day that Tiffany's body was found, I called my father, sobbing.

"Don't let yourself get all upset over it," he told me. "She had a stinking rotten life. Everyone crapped on her, but what's done is done."

Days later, again on the phone, he was recounting some incident or other and said, "After your sister was...vanquished, I gave it some more thought."

It was such a strange word to use: *vanquished*. Defeated.

Among her papers we found a letter she'd written to our father. In it she apologized for killing herself and thanked him for everything he had done for her.

There can't be anything worse than losing a child, but on some level mustn't our father have been relieved? This person who calls you on the phone every morning and harangues you, threatens you, is gone now. The car alarm that was your daughter is finally shut off, the cable cut.

In the wake of her death, we still think of her accusations. Our father could certainly be inappropriate, especially when held to today's standards, but that didn't necessarily make him a pedophile. That said, his behavior didn't help his case any. To the rest of us, it was, if not normal, then at least *him*—the way he'd take us to McDonald's, for instance, and say to the counter girl if she was overweight, "Well, hey there, Porky."

"Dad," we'd say, so embarrassed.

He'd just laugh. "She's out of shape, and someone needs to tell her as much."

If a woman was sexy, he'd point that out as well. And if one was ugly, he'd wince, the way you might if you were witnessing an accident. That was the worst, as far as he was concerned. "There's nothing…feminine there," he'd gripe, recalling some bank teller or supermarket cashier who hadn't met his standard. "Nothing of beauty."

He always monitored my sisters' weight and appearance. When Lisa was sixty-three she told our father that she'd lost twenty pounds. "And you know what he said?" she asked. "'Lose any more and you and me are going to have a love affair.'"

"That's a great incentive!" I said. "Slim down to one-fifty and you finally get to have sex with a ninety-five-year-old man who is also your father!"

"I have the most beautiful girls on the block," he'd boast

back in the seventies and early eighties. "By far. No one else even comes close."

At the country club, members would approach our table. "What good-looking daughters you have, Lou." I'd sit there in my red, white, and blue American flag tie, my glasses, my braces, and think that with very little effort they could have tossed my brother and me a bone, could have upped that to "good-looking *family*." It was true, though. My sisters were beautiful. Part of me was envious, but mainly I was proud. Families where the daughters are ugly don't count. I learned that early on. We all did.

I think of us together at the country club on prime-rib night. The girls—Dad's prizes—dressed up, his eyes on them as they glided to the buffet and back, making sure they didn't overdo it with the ambrosia salad. I think of Tiffany. Not long ago I was in a hotel dining room. I'd finished my meal and approached a group of strangers: a mother, a dad, and four kids ranging in age from twelve to eighteen, all nicely dressed and groomed, none of them on their phones, all of them lively and engaged. "What a beautiful family you have," I said to the parents. Then, times being what they are and afraid that I had crossed some line, I hurried, awkwardly, out the door and back to my room.

Smile, Beautiful

A month into New York City's stay-at-home order, I took an afternoon walk and fell in behind a man who was heading up Madison Avenue. The guy was a few inches taller than me, unremarkable in terms of his clothing, and I wouldn't have paid him any mind had he not cleared his throat and spat onto the sidewalk. I was just glaring at it—the nerve of some people!—when a young woman turned the corner and headed in our direction. Like me, she had a mask on, so it surprised me when the man called out, "Hey, beautiful. Smile, why don't you?"

Did you really just say that? I wanted to ask. First off, for all he knew she *was* smiling, and, secondly, hadn't the #MeToo movement taught even the most boorish of us that women hate being told what to do with their faces?

I couldn't stand wearing a mask. It made the city smell like my breath, which hinted of milk with some house paint mixed in. I was bothered by the sameness it engendered. Central Park, the Lower East Side, the Greek neighborhood in Queens where I buy my cheese, Coney Island—they all smelled exactly alike now.

My mask at that time was blue gingham. It was given to me by my sister Amy and was made to fit a small woman rather than a slightly less small man. The fabric was agreeable, but the straps, which were too tight, caused my ears to stick out and look like Pringles on hinges.

Still, I reminded myself, I was not the only one suffering. Whenever I couldn't bear it for another moment, I'd think of all the people who might have actually welcomed a mask—this woman I once read about in a book, for example. She was on a tour of Antarctica, and when she bent down on the ice to admire a baby leopard seal, it leapt up and bit her nose off. The whole thing. So a face mask, for her, would likely have been welcome. For the first time in years she'd look just like everyone else she passed on the street. It was the same for people with cleft palates, or remarkably weak chins.

I'm terribly self-conscious about my teeth, so for me the mask offered a welcome break from the judgment I so often felt in the United States. *I'm not sure you belong here,* I could sense the clerks thinking in fancy shops and hotels. *If you really had money, wouldn't you spend a little of it in a dentist's office?* It could have been worse, I supposed. My teeth were mostly present and accounted for. Still I'd be fooling myself to think they weren't the first thing people noticed about me.

It wasn't always this way. I had braces when I was young, and when they were removed at age seventeen or so, I looked fantastic. Then I ruined everything by not wearing my retainer the way I was supposed to. By the age of twenty I noticed a slight gap between my front teeth, one that widened significantly with the passage of time. I could slip a credit card in there, then a credit card atop a library card. Then the edge of my wallet. Next I developed gaps between the teeth that *neighbored* the front ones. There's only so much space in my top jaw, so the incisors started jutting out. "You look like you swallowed a bomb and your face froze a fraction of a second after it went off," Amy told me.

What do people without sisters do? Turn to someone like my friend Scott. "You have summer teeth," he once told me.

I said, "Excuse me?"

"Summer here, summer there," he explained.

A person who's not me might have realized this on his own, but I can't look at my open mouth. It's the only certified phobia I have. When the pandemic started I had not seen my teeth in close to forty years. In pictures I'd smile broadly but with my lips together, like a Peanuts character, and I would never watch a video of myself.

When conversing, I tend to cover my mouth, especially if the other person has beautiful teeth, which are always the first thing I notice about someone. Even pets. "Poor thing," a friend once said of his cat. "Cromwell just went to the vet and had all of his premolars and canines removed."

Ha ha, I thought, feeling so superior. To a cat.

* * *

America is a hard place to be if you're self-conscious about your smile—especially certain parts of America, like Southern California. I used to think that people there wore dark glasses because it was hard to drive with the sun in their eyes. More likely it's the glare of an oncoming driver's teeth that blinds them. This is why I feel so comfortable in Japan, where dental standards are seemingly nonexistent and people have been wearing masks for years. The scariest mouth I ever saw was on a clerk in a Tokyo department store. The woman's top central incisors grew outward from her gums like tusks and formed a dark, uneven shelf her upper lip rested upon.

I said to an oral surgeon in London, "You'd think that a Japanese dentist might have helped her out for no money, just as a project."

"Someone most likely offered to," he said. "But when a person is that far gone, it's usually the result of a phobia. They won't go in for treatment, even if it's free."

The surgeon's theory was tested a few weeks later, in West Sussex. I was at a thrift shop in a village near my house. The clerk was young and cheerful, and when he opened his mouth to greet me I was struck by what were easily the second-worst teeth I have ever seen. Some were broken off while others were missing. There were gray ones and black ones, this one straight and the next at an odd angle, like a mouthful of pebbles—startling, in part, because he was otherwise so nice-looking. It was a lot to take in, and I thought that surely he could feel my eyes focusing on that part of his face, just as someone with an unfortunately placed birthmark might.

I can be pretty impulsive, which is dangerous when you couple it with an outsized disposable income. "Oh, what the hell," I said not long ago, agreeing to a $3,000 heavy black sport coat with layers of ruffles spilling from the hem. Need I mention that it didn't fit me and never will unless I have *all* of my ribs removed?

My impulsiveness extends to others as well. At a book signing once, I started asking people if they spoke a foreign language. This was in Reno, Nevada, a city whose charms are not obvious to the casual observer. "I speak a little Spanish," someone would say, or, "I had a semester of German in college."

Eventually I met a young woman who'd taken six years of French. She had come to my event alone and was exactly the sort of reader I dreamed of when I first started writing.

"Have you been to Paris?" I asked.

She said no, and when I asked why not, she gave me the same look I'd have given myself forty years earlier. "I'm a barista with student debt. There's no way I can afford a plane ticket halfway around the world."

"Then I'm going to buy you one," I said.

When Hugh was the age this young woman was, he went to Paris alone and decided that he'd rather die than return home. He started taking French classes and eventually found work as a cook for an elderly couple. That led to friendships and other jobs—a whole life. I imagined the same thing happening to this young woman. All she needed was someone to open the door.

This, I've always thought, is the whole purpose of having money: to change people's lives.

"But who were you to decide her life *needed* changing?" Hugh asked when I told him about her. "You knew her for all of five minutes."

The young woman waited six months to earn what she considered to be a decent amount of spending money. Then she got on the plane and flew to Paris. A few days into her stay she went to a café with a view of Notre Dame and sent me an email. In it she said that she had arrived safely and would give anything to be back in Reno, sitting on her front porch and drinking Jack Daniel's with a pickle juice chaser. The trip I had financed had indeed taught her a lesson: There's no place like home.

This was not the first time I'd done something like this. Neither would it be the last. Of course, when someone *asks* for my help, I rarely give it, deciding that it needs to be *my* idea. I thought about the young man at the charity shop for a couple of weeks before I returned one afternoon and pulled him aside. "Listen," I said, "I don't want to embarrass you, and I know how strange this is going to sound, but I'd like to pay to have your teeth fixed. I don't want anything in return—you and I don't ever need to speak again. We can set this up with a local dentist. He or she will send me the bills, and I'll see to them."

The young man blinked.

"You're what," I guessed, "twenty-three years old?"

"Twenty-four," he told me.

"The point is that you have your whole life ahead of you," I continued. "This could change everything."

I'd realize only later how suspect I sounded. Before stopping in at the charity shop, I'd been picking up litter by the side of the road. And so I was dressed like I lived outside. My shirt, which was untucked and torn, was stained with dirt and dried blood that came from reaching deep into blackberry bushes for the empty bottles and cans people deposit there. My arms were scratched, as was my neck. I looked and smelled like I'd been fighting a cheetah over an antelope carcass. Then there were the contents of my own mouth, the teeth spaced like tombstones in a church graveyard. *If you want to pay for someone's dental work, you might want to start with your own,* the young man, whom I'll call Denton, was probably thinking.

"Well," he said, "a lady I talked to once mentioned something about dentures —"

"You don't want dentures," I told him. "They're a pain in the ass. Implants, though — it's amazing what they can do now. Please, let me take care of this for you." I wrote down my name and email address. "I know how crazy this sounds, believe me."

He took the slip of paper I offered. "I don't know what to say."

I shrugged. "Say yes."

"And you honestly thought he'd take you up on it?" my friend Adam asked a few months later when I told him about it.

"Well…sure," I said. "I mean, an offer like that is only going to come once in a lifetime."

He laughed. "That might be true, but you sounded like an old pervert."

Hugh was of the same opinion.

"But I specifically told him I *didn't* want anything in return," I said in my defense, realizing as the words left my mouth that that's exactly what an old pervert *would* say, especially one with scratch marks on his neck and dried blood on his shirt. "Still, he could have googled me," I argued. "I've never looked myself up, but surely there must be something about me online that's positive, or at least not so horribly negative that someone wouldn't trust me to pay for his implants."

I haven't been back to the charity shop since the afternoon when I offered my help, and probably won't return in the future. Twice I've passed Denton on the street, and though we nod hello to each other, it's definitely weird. I don't want to make things worse by pressing him, though I often think of what a difference this could have made in his life. Then again, who am I to decide that his life needs improving? He immediately struck me as a genuinely decent person, so maybe his friends and family—the ones who really matter—look at him and see only that: his goodness.

Just when I felt certain that I'd never hear from Denton, the pandemic hit. If wearing a mask changed the way the world saw *me*—someone who, given my age, is more or less invisible—I could only imagine what it had done for him. To talk to people and not notice them zeroing in on your mouth, to have them look you in the eye and think, *Hey, who's he?* That had to feel good to him. I know it did to me. So much so that when dentists' offices reopened, I went to one in New York, a Greek woman recommended by a friend, and got braces—at age sixty-four. They weren't the metal kind I'd worn as a teenager but a new type made of clear plastic. Invisalign, they're called, and I first heard of them through my niece. She'd gotten them herself and explained that every two weeks she put in a new pair and threw out the old ones.

"Can you give them to me to wear?" I asked. In the dumb-question department this is right up there with "Do you think mankind might one day live peacefully on the sun?"

The first step in getting my own Invisaligns was having my mouth scanned. This was done by a technician with a wand that seemed designed for a much larger mouth, a lion's perhaps. The result was a 3D image of my teeth and gums that the dentist could manipulate, showing me what I would look like after only fourteen weeks of treatment. My spring lecture tours had been canceled, so it wasn't like I needed to be anywhere or do an excessive amount of talking. And I'd need to wear them only on top. So why not?

The Invisaligns arrived in early April—seven installments' worth, each in its own plastic envelope with a date written on it. Every other Thursday I was to pop in a new one and wear it for a minimum of twenty-two hours a day, basically just removing it for meals. The first time you put a new one in, your teeth say, and loudly, *"WHAT THE FUCK DO YOU THINK*

YOU'RE DOING?" They pipe down after a few hours, though. I'd worried I might talk funny, but the difference was hardly profound. At the worst I sounded slightly drunk.

I was born without my left lateral incisor, and my teenage braces had pushed everything together, thus eliminating the empty space. Now the plan was to remake that empty space and fill it with a fake tooth. Even with my Play-Doh gums, it was startling how quickly my teeth seemed to be moving. I could feel the change with my tongue but still couldn't bring myself to look.

"What are you so afraid of?" Hugh asked. "I mean, honestly, so what if your teeth are black?"

I panicked. "Are they?"

"Why don't you see for yourself?"

But I couldn't, not even when the dentist urged me to during a mid-Invisalign checkup.

"What's going on with these molars?" she asked, poking around toward the back of my mouth. "They seem to be awfully flat."

"Like a cow's?"

She thought for a moment. "Or a donkey's."

Ah, Greeks.

The fourteen weeks passed quickly and without incident. The braces cost more in time than they did in money. They're clear, so I spent untold hours looking for where I'd left them. On the bedspread, on the desk, atop a dirty T-shirt of Hugh's with Snoopy on it—they blended right in, chameleon-like. On the appointed date I returned to the dentist, who seemed happy with the way everything had shifted. That afternoon my gap would be plugged with a false tooth, and crowns would be fitted on its three closest neighbors. In order to apply them, three incisors had to be filed to thin, sharp posts, resembling, I imagine, the teeth of a baby alligator. "I never let people look at themselves in this condition," the dentist said. "If they tell me they have to go to the bathroom, I say, 'Sorry, but you'll have to hold it.' Because shaved-down teeth—what you have in your mouth right now—are impossible to *unsee* once you've seen them."

I was in the chair for close to three hours, and at the end of the session, when the dentist handed me the mirror, I held it in front of me, screwed up my courage, and opened my mouth. All I had ever wanted was for the sight to be unremarkable. Not perfect or blinding, but ordinary for a man my age.

"What were his teeth like?" someone might ask.

And you would answer, "Gosh, I didn't notice. Terrible bags under his eyes, though."

What I saw before me was a step up from unremarkable, though maybe my assessment will change with time. As it was, the view was clouded with pride, the sort you feel when you refinish a piece of furniture or renovate a kitchen, though in this case I'd done none of the work myself, just ordered it to be done, and put up with the slight discomfort while it was going on.

"Now let me show you your 'before' pictures," the dentist

said. She pulled out her phone and I saw what looked to be the mouth of a hippo in attack mode. Summer teeth indeed. How had I chewed food?

"And I was walking around like that?" I asked.

She put her phone away. "Apparently."

My new teeth must have looked amazing when, a few minutes later, the receptionist presented me with a $14,000 bill for one day's work and my mouth dropped open.

Back at the apartment, I smiled at Hugh so broadly that my eyes disappeared.

Hugh considered me. "I liked you better before."

Amy said the same thing. "Your old teeth had character."

"Yes, but you didn't have to *live* with them," I told her. "The guy who pushes himself along on a dolly has character too, but that doesn't mean he shouldn't get a set of functioning legs if he wants them."

Amy had come to our apartment for a celebratory dinner. Hugh made spaghetti, and it was the first time in forty years I could put a forkful in my mouth and cleanly bite it off, just like a normal person. In the past, the strands would get caught in my gaps and I had to really gnaw at them, the way a dog might.

It took a while for me to stop covering my mouth when I spoke. *Hold on*, I'd think, looking at the teeth of whoever I was talking to. *If anyone needs to be embarrassed, it's* him.

I noticed too how having unremarkable teeth boosted my confidence. Now, when my credit card didn't go through, I'd say calmly, "Maybe if you try it again." In the past I'd immediately start sweating, not because I'd done anything wrong but because my gaps made me look like I had. I felt more comfortable checking into a nice hotel. I felt like a slate had been wiped clean, and now the world could judge me for the shitty things I said rather than the shitty way I looked while saying them.

When told by a woman at a book signing that I had a beautiful smile, I seriously thought I might cry. Never did I expect to hear that from someone. It would have been like getting a compliment on my hair, which would happen only if the rest of the world suddenly went bald and I now had something they didn't.

How silly of me not to have done this sooner. I'd thought it would take years, that I'd be one of those unfortunate adults with a mouthful of metal, but in fact it was three and a half months from start to finish, which is nothing.

I think of that young man in England, the one with his whole life ahead of him. I think of what my most recent dental work cost altogether. Next I double it, calculating what I'd have paid had both my top *and* bottom teeth needed attention. Then I pray that he lost the slip of paper I wrote my name and email address on.

Pussytoes

Ten days before my father died, he suffered a small stroke and fell. Or perhaps he fell and then had the stroke. Either way, it surprised me when people asked what was the cause of death. I mean, he was ninety-eight! Wasn't that cause enough?

I visited him shortly after his fall, flew down from New York with Amy and Hugh. Gretchen and Paul met us at Springmoor, but he was essentially gone by then. There was a livid gash on his forehead, and he was propped up in his bed, which seemed ridiculously short, like a cut-down one you'd see in a department store. His eyes were closed, his mouth was open, and behind his lips swayed a glistening curtain of spittle.

"Dad?" Amy said.

An aide entered and shook his leg. "Mr. Sedaris? Lou? You got some family here to see you." She looked at us, then back at our father. "He pretty much be this way now." Another shake of the leg. "Mr. Sedaris?"

In response our father gasped for breath.

"Well, he *looks* good," Amy said, pulling a chair up to his bedside.

Who is she comparing him to? I wondered. Google "old man dying," and I'm pretty sure you'll see exactly what was in front of us: an unconscious skeleton with just a little meat on it, moaning.

You always think that if you gather round and really concentrate, the person on the bed will let go. *We were all there,* you imagine yourself saying to friends. *And in an odd way, it was sort of beautiful.* So you become solemn and silently sit, watching the chest unsteadily rise and fall. You look at the hands as they occasionally stir, doing some imaginary last-minute busywork. The oxygen tube slips, and though you think of readjusting it, you don't, because, well, it has snot on it. *Better to save it for an aide,* you tell yourself. After twenty or so minutes your sister Gretchen steps outside. Then Hugh leaves the room, followed by Paul. You go out yourself and find them all gathered in the open-air courtyard, seated in rocking chairs, Gretchen lighting a cigarette. "Did I tell you we're not allowed to say *native plants* at work anymore?" she asks.

A horticulturist for the city of Raleigh, she's the only one in the family with a real job, meaning a boss she has to report to and innumerable, pointless meetings that eat up her valuable time. Gretchen talks about work a lot, but I'm always happy to hear it. "What did you say when they told you that?" I ask.

"Nothing," she tells me. "I just walked out. I mean, it's ridiculous!"

A minute later Amy joins us.

"Now people are calling for gender-neutral toilets in the city parks," Gretchen is saying. "There's not enough in the budget to build them, so most likely the few bathrooms that already exist will wind up being labeled as unisex. I guess this solves the problem, but I *like* having a separate women's room." She crushes her cigarette. "Men's bathrooms always smell like shit."

"And the women's smell like vomit," Amy says.

"Do they really?" I ask, wondering if my father might die while we're all sitting outside, talking about how public toilets smell.

"God, yes," Gretchen says. She reaches into her purse and pulls out a palm-sized black book. "Here." She hands it to me. "I found this at Dad's house a few days ago and saved it for you."

I mistake it for a pocket Bible, super-abbreviated, with only the good parts included, and just as I wonder, *Wait—what good parts?* I realize it's for addresses, that it is, true to its color and size, my father's Little Black Book. "It must have been from before he went to Syracuse and started writing in all capital letters," Gretchen says.

I open it to find fifty or so names, followed by addresses and phone numbers, mainly of women, and most with a note beside them:

Faith Avery—Too serious!
Beryl Davis—YES!
Dorothy Castle—Short circuit
Edna Hallenbeck—WOW!
Helen Wasto—Beautiful
Pat Smith—Body!!!!!
Mary Hobart—Advanced
Helen Sampson—The Greatest!!
Arlene Knickerbocker—Looks are deceiving
Fredericka Montague—Lovely!
Patty O'Day—Beauty!!! Personality
Ann Quinlan—Body! That's all!! No brains
Rose Stevens—Aaahh

Returning to the room, I look at my father, still seemingly asleep, and wonder if he had sex with these women or just tried to. Why were none of them Greek, and what does *advanced* mean? I bring it up with Hugh a few hours later, after we've left Springmoor and are on our way to the beach. "If Patty O'Day and Dorothy Castle are still alive, do you think they remember him?"

"I guess it depends on what went on," Hugh says. "Anyway, I'm sure you can ask your father about it the next time you see him."

We pass a low brick house with a tattered TRUMP flag in its front yard. "The next time I see him, he'll be dead," I say.

Hugh frowns. "You don't know that. I mean, he's pulled through before."

This was on a Sunday in late May. Six days later, Springmoor called and said that my father had stopped eating and was on morphine. My sister Lisa and her husband, Bob, were at the Sea Section with us by then, as was my friend Ronnie and Hugh's friend Carol. We all went to dinner that night in the town of Atlantic Beach. "Dad is going to die while we're eating," I said as we left the house. It was a hot, humid evening, more summer than spring.

"David!" Hugh scolded.

"I'm not wishing," I told him, "just predicting."

And correctly, it turned out. Lisa received the call just as we were finishing our appetizers. There was no music playing at the Island Grille, but because the room was small and filled to capacity, it was too loud to hear the Springmoor representative on the other end. Lisa stepped outside, and I followed a few minutes later. "Dad's dead," she said matter-of-factly as I closed the screen door behind me.

She was seated on a bench, and as I took the spot beside her, a young couple left the restaurant hand in hand and headed toward their car, stopping beneath a streetlamp along the way to kiss. The man was thin and bearded, a good deal taller than the young woman. As she stood on her toes to reach his mouth, her skirt rose high enough to expose her underwear. "Look at what that girl is wearing," Lisa said, the phone still in her lap, half of Paul's number pushed into it.

"It's certainly short," I said, following her eyes. "But it works for her."

Lisa let out a breath and finished dialing. "If you say so."

She told Paul that our father had died, and I told the others. It's something you think about all your life—getting a call like that. *When will it happen, and where will I be?* you wonder. There's a responsibility in delivering such news, but the more times you phone and get someone's voice mail, the less solemn you're likely to be. In the end I sounded pissed off more than anything. "Where have you *been*? Dad's dead."

Gretchen was particularly hard to contact, and I didn't reach her until the following morning. We talked for a while, and she called me back a few hours later, sounding almost stoned. "I'm just wandering around in a daze," she said.

"I hear that's fairly normal," I told her, looking out the sliding glass door at the ocean, which was relatively calm and green.

"I mean...I could be coming into some real money!" she continued.

And so, for her, I was the bearer of *good* news.

When our mother died, my siblings and I fell headfirst into a dark pit. Those first few days were the blackest. It was the same after our sister Tiffany's suicide. With our father, though, it was different. By the time the check arrived at the Island Grille that night, we were talking about other things: gas stoves versus electric ones, a funny TV show about vampires, the time Lisa ate an entire gallon of ice cream with her bare hands while driving home from the grocery store, clawing it out of the carton with her increasingly numb fingers. Perhaps we strayed so easily onto other topics because, at my father's advanced age, this moment was expected. Then too he was Lou Sedaris. By the second half of his ninety-seventh year, the man was a pussycat, a delight. Unfortunately there were all those years that preceded it. The world didn't slow down for his death, much less stop—not even for us, his family.

A month before our father's stroke, Amy and I went through a box of pictures and chose what we thought might make the perfect obituary photo: Dad at his fiftieth birthday party, standing in his basement with a ghutra on his head. It might have been a white dishcloth, but the band that held it in place was convincing, as was his tanned skin and clasped hands. He looked like a Saudi diplomat on a short break from brokering a peace deal or ordering the murder of a journalist. Our second runner-up was of him wearing long, thin Willie Nelson braids. They were fake, attached to a headband, and had been put on him by Paul. The pictures made him appear much more fun than he actually was. They did him a favor.

"Ummm, no," Lisa said when the time came to contact the newspaper. "I want something that people will be able to recognize." The one she chose amounted to an old person's senior class photo, a snapshot of our father at age ninety-six, withered and lost-looking, taken at Springmoor.

This is how resentments can build after someone dies:

one decision at a time. The obituary was similarly bland—a résumé, essentially. Not that I wanted to write it. Neither did Paul or Gretchen or Amy. None of us could have managed the countless things Lisa saw to: contacting the funeral home; clearing out our father's room at Springmoor; calling his bank, his lawyer. He wanted a funeral at the Greek Orthodox Church. This meant that he couldn't be cremated, so a casket had to be purchased and clothing picked out.

Most people I know would prefer to be disposed of with as little fanfare as possible. My English friend Andrew, for example, has donated his body to science. "I read an account somewhere or other of medical students using an old woman's intestines as a skipping rope," he told me not long after he'd made his arrangements. "It shocked me at first, but I'll be dead when the time comes, so I probably won't mind it so much."

Andrew wants no church service but wouldn't object if a few people got together for drinks or a nice meal in his memory. My father, by contrast, insisted on what amounted to a three-part multistate death tour. As I said to Gretchen, "It's a lot of running around for someone who couldn't be bothered to pick us up from the airport."

There was to be a funeral in Raleigh, a burial almost a week later in my father's hometown of Cortland, New York, then a third service to take place forty days after his death, a sort of "Don't think for one minute that you can forget me" sort of thing, after which a traditional dish of boiled wheat berries and pomegranate would be served.

Greek Orthodox funerals, like Catholic ones, are essentially Masses. My father's took place at Holy Trinity—the church we grew up in—on a Tuesday morning. Paul lives in Raleigh, and Gretchen works there. They could have easily driven to the service from their homes, but instead we all checked into a hotel, a very expensive one, in the town of Cary, and really pushed the boat out, charging everything to the estate: room service, drinks—the works. The staff thought we were attending a wedding, that's how merry we seemed as we headed to the church in our dress clothes. "Can you take our picture?" Amy asked one of the doormen as she handed him her phone. She looked like she was going to a ball thrown by Satan. The dress she wore was black but short, with comically massive sleeves. It was textured like a thick paper towel and was definitely not mournful. Paul, by contrast, looked like he worked at an ice cream parlor.

"Dad's casket is cherry with brushed nickel trim," Lisa informed us as we took our spots in the front pew. "And just so you know, I had him dressed in his underwear, not a diaper. With regular pants over them, of course."

"Uh...great," we said, wondering how the coffin she'd selected could possibly have been any uglier. If it was a chair, it would have been high-backed and upholstered in burgundy-colored corduroy. If it was a lamp, it would have had a frosted hurricane shade. Just as the service began, two men in suits lifted the casket's lid, revealing our father from the sternum up. What struck me, what struck us all, was how tiny he was. His hands—seemingly no larger than a ventriloquist's dummy's—rested vampirically across his chest while his face and hair were the spooky off-white of a button mushroom, with a mushroom's slight sheen as well. He looked, in Amy's words, "like he was carved out of makeup."

"That open-casket business is so tacky," I said afterward as we gathered for coffee and baklava in the church's multi-purpose room. "If I had to go on display after my death, I'd at least demand that they position me facedown. Then there'd just be the back of my head to worry about."

Actually I'd love to be cremated in a simple pine box painted by Hugh with the image or pattern of his choice. I honestly think that would be the perfect business for him. "People could live with their coffins for years, using them as blanket chests or bookshelves—even coffee tables," I said as we left the funeral. "A-Tisket, A-Casket, the company could be called."

Our hotel was near a state park, and after changing into our post-funeral outfits, Amy, Gretchen, and I walked to it. The afternoon was hot and bright. On our way over, we passed a furious stick figure of a man who stood beside a dog carrier and an overstuffed sack of clothing, angrily shaking a hand-written sign at the approaching cars. He wore no shirt and had tattoos on his arms and the backs of his hands. People had given him food and water, and the empty bags and plastic bottles littered the ground around him. On our approach we could see the lean-to he'd set up in a thicket, and that too was overspilling with trash.

This got Gretchen to talk about the camps she and her crews find on city property. "It's sad," she said, "but if we don't clear them out, it's just one phone call after another, with people complaining about human shit and needles."

It was nice to reach the park and escape the cruel sun, which was now blocked by a high, brilliant canopy of leaves. It felt ten degrees cooler in the forest. It felt like the funeral was far behind us. We'd been walking for ten or so minutes when Gretchen suddenly stopped and knelt before a number of small plants with ragged white blossoms on them. "Look," she cried, "pussytoes!"

"They're *what*?" I asked.

"*Antennaria plantaginifolia*," she said. "Pussytoes."

"Oh, that is going to be my password for *everything* from this moment on," Amy told us. As she pulled out her phone to make a note, it rang and she answered with a luminous, "Hi, Dad!"

She said it so brightly and naturally that I honestly believed for one crazy moment that this had all been a prank, that the body we'd seen at the church had indeed been a double carved out of makeup, and that our father was still alive. And I thought, *Fuck!*

Following my mother's death, had a sorceress said, "I'll bring her back, *but*—," I'd have said, "Yes!" without even waiting for the rest of the sentence. And if Mom and I had twenty more years together, her being herself and me being, say, a deaf mouse who had to live in her underpants, I'd still have counted it as a fair exchange.

My father, though, was a different story. One of the things

I'd heard again and again at the church that morning was "Lou was a real character."

A *character* is what you call a massively difficult person once he has reached the age of eighty-five. It's what Hitler might have been labeled had he lived another three decades, and Idi Amin. But there's a role you have to play when a parent dies, so I'd said, each time I'd heard it, "Yes, he certainly was unique."

"I know you're going to miss him terribly" was another often repeated line.

"Oh, goodness, yes," I'd say—not a lie, exactly. I think I'll miss him the same way I missed getting colds during the pandemic, but who knows how I might feel a few years down the line?

It used to be that people's parents died in their sixties and seventies, cleanly, of good old-fashioned cancers and heart attacks, meaning the child was on his or her own by the age of forty-five or so. Now, though, with people living longer and longer, you can be a grandparent and still be somebody's son or daughter. The woman across the road from us in Normandy was eighty when her mother died—eighty! That, to me, is terrifying. It's disfiguring to be a child for that long, or at least it is if your relationship with that parent is troubled. For years I'd felt like one of those pollarded plane trees I'll forever associate with Paris, the sort that's been brutally pruned since saplinghood and in winter resembles a towering fist.

As long as my father had power, he used it to hurt me. In my youth I just took it. Then I started to write about it, to actually profit from it. The money was a comfort, but better yet was the roar of live audiences as they laughed at how petty and arrogant he was.

"Well, I feel sorry for him," Hugh has taken to saying. "Nobody was born acting the way he did. Something must have happened that made him that mean."

This is true, but getting to the root of my father was virtually impossible. He never answered questions about his youth, saying only "What do you want to know *that* for?"

During one of the many prayer breaks at his funeral, on my knees but with my eyes open, I remembered the time I was invited to give the baccalaureate address at Princeton. Those things are difficult to write, at least for me. The audience is always exhausted, it's always unbearably hot out, and on top of it all, you're forced to wear a dark, heavy robe and what looks like a cushion on your head. I was going to decline the offer, but instead I called my father and said that if he would like to accompany me, I'd do it. The Ivy League stuff really appealed to him—though, in fairness, it always has to me as well. People who attended Harvard or Princeton or Yale are always maddeningly discreet about it. "I went to school in the Boston area," they say, or, "I think I spent some time in New Jersey once." Had I graduated from a top-notch school, I'd have found a way to work it into every conversation I had:

"Would you like that coffee hot or iced?"

"Back at Columbia I always had it hot, but what the hell, let's try something new."

Now my father said, "Princeton! Are you kidding! I'd love to go."

Before the graduation ceremony, we attended a luncheon and sat at a table with the president of the university. There were other people joining us, dignitaries of one stripe or another, and as our food was delivered, my father—who had earlier referred to Bill Clinton, who would be speaking the following day, as "Slick Willie"—told the president that she had made a terrible mistake. "You asked my son to give this speech, but the person you really want is my daughter Amy. She'd have the audience in the palm of her hand. They'd eat her up, I'm telling you. I've got videotapes I can send you, her on some of the talk shows. Then you'll see! Amy's the ticket, not David."

The university president politely thanked him for his suggestion. Then she asked me a question about the lecture tour I had just wrapped up, and my father started in again. "I can see the graduates and their families right now. They'd go home talking about her! They'd tell all their friends! Amy's who you want."

"Is this why you came here with me?" I asked him afterward, as a car arrived to take us to New York.

"Oh, don't pull that business," my father said. "The woman needed to know that she could have done better."

I was fifty years old at the time, and what hurt were not my father's words—I was immune by this point—but the fact that he was still trying to undermine me. I never blamed Amy when things like this happened. It wasn't her fault. Likewise, I never blamed Gretchen when I had an art show and he told whoever was in charge that the person they really needed was his daughter Gretchen. "She's got the talent, not him."

He was always trying to pit his children against one another, never understanding the bond we shared. It was forged by having him as a father, and as long as he was alive, it held. One always hears of families falling apart after the death of a parent. Lifelong checks are no longer in place and the balance is thrown off. Slights become insurmountable. There are squabbles over the estate, etc. It's a pretty rough patch of road.

Saul Bellow wrote, "Losing a parent is something like driving through a plate-glass window. You didn't know it was there until it shattered, and then for years to come you're picking up the pieces." I felt like I'd collected all the big, easy-to-reach, obvious ones. The splinters, though, will definitely take a while—the rest of my life, perhaps. I could feel them beneath my skin as I paused with my sisters in this cool, shady glen, orphaned at last among the pussytoes.

Lucky-Go-Happy

Throughout the worst of the pandemic I, like everyone, thought of the many things I'd failed to appreciate back when life was normal: oh, to be handed an actual restaurant menu; to stand so close to a stranger that you can read the banal text messages that are obviously more important to him than his toddler stumbling off the curb and out into traffic.

Many felt that they had taken their jobs for granted, but not me. I always loved my work, or at least the part of it that was public and involved reading out loud. The last show I did before COVID robbed me of my livelihood was in Vancouver, British Columbia, in a theater I didn't much care for, a rock house with a grim, cramped lobby and the sort of dressing room you see in movies about performers who overdose on drugs because their dressing rooms are so depressing. The audience was lovely, though, and I liked my hotel, which, at the end of

243

the day, is really what it's all about. I'm never the one paying for the room, so I'm spared the part where you lie awake and wonder if it's really worth six or seven or eight hundred dollars just so someone can creep in while you're out and arrange a pair of slippers beside your freshly turned-down bed. They're on the carpet and look like they belong to a wealthy ghost who's just scooted over to make room for you.

In the restaurant of my Vancouver hotel the following morning, I sat beside a handsome actor it took me no time at all to recognize. On the television series I had most recently watched him in, he was quick-tempered and physically abusive, so I liked how polite he was to the waiter and to the woman who floated away with his empty orange-juice glass. "Oh, thanks. That's very kind of you."

As I boarded the elevator back to my room, the hotel manager stepped in and asked me how my stay was going. "Terrific," I told him. "I just saw a big star in the restaurant."

"I can't confirm that," the fellow said, offering a stiff smile.

"I don't need you to," I told him, offering a smile of my own. "I know perfectly well who it was."

Then I couldn't remember the guy's name for the life of me. "Oh, you know," I said to my friend Adam, who had produced the previous evening's event and rode with me to the airport an hour or so after I had finished my breakfast. "It was what's his name who's on that TV series with the woman who used to be married to the guy who made that movie with a song in it that everybody knows."

Aside from my star sighting, my last show was pretty

typical. I read something new and realized it didn't work as well as I'd hoped. Then I signed books for three hours. The evening was unremarkable—a shame, as for the next year and a half I would think back on it obsessively, would almost fetishize it. *That was what I used to do for a living,* I'd think. *And now it's over.* On the best days I'd remind myself that everyone was sitting at home, that this was just a temporary setback. A part of me worried, though, that when the world eventually moved on, it would do so without me, or at least without any particular need of me. The circus would take to the road again, but not with this elephant.

I decided from the start of the pandemic not to get Zoom. "What do you mean, 'get' it?" Hugh asked. "It's nothing you have to buy or attach to your computer. You press a button and, wham, it's there."

"Well, can you mark which button?" I asked. "I want to make sure I never push it."

Over the course of the next eighteen months, I did do one Zoom event, though it wasn't on my computer. Rather, someone came to the apartment, and I used his instead.

"How did it go?" my lecture agent asked when it was over.

"I have no idea," I told him. And it was true. Without out a live audience—that unwitting congregation of fail-safe editors—I'm lost. It's not just their laughter I pay attention to but also the quality of their silence. As for noises, a groan is always good in my opinion. A cough means that if they were reading this passage on the page, they'd be skimming now, while a snore is your brother-in-law putting a gun to your head and pulling the trigger.

Of course, I wrote during the pandemic. I published things, which was scary, as without a public reading I had no idea whether they actually worked or not. I can occasionally try something out on Hugh but not for long. At most he'll listen for a minute or so before turning away and saying he'd rather read whatever it is himself, and only after the book or magazine comes out in print.

"Yes, but by then it'll be too late to make changes," I tell him.

Hugh and I have vastly different senses of humor—this is to say that I have one and he doesn't. What I need him for are the *You can't say that*s and *You're disgusting*s he'll interrupt me with on the few occasions that I make it beyond my opening paragraph.

Hugh saying, "That's terrible," is a sure sign that an audience will laugh. One of my many nicknames for him is Congressman Prude, and for good reason. "I just don't see the need for that language," he'll sniff, meaning, on one occasion, the term *bare bottom,* and, on another, *ovaries.* "Do you have to talk that way?"

To be on tour was to hear at least ten times a day, "You must be exhausted." People would insist that what I was going through was grossly unfair, too much to ask of a mortal human, and just as I'd find myself agreeing, I'd think, *Hold on…all I've actually done this morning is eat breakfast and take an hour-long flight from Atlanta to Birmingham. That's not at all exhausting.* There were days, certainly, when it was stressful. Flights would be canceled and alternatives hastily configured. But it wasn't *me* doing the configuring. Rather, it was a travel agent, a professional. I'd see hotheads in those long customer-service lines, the ones in which every passenger required a full half hour of phone calls and concentrated keyboard pecking, but that was never me. I outsourced the drama to someone else, so even when it led to a hectic rerouting, I couldn't really complain.

I flew a dozen or so times during the worst of the pandemic—to North Carolina, to Indiana and Kentucky, to the UK. It pained me to see the airports so empty, a majority of the businesses shuttered, the lounges closed. While walking through Charlotte Douglas International one afternoon in the summer of 2020, I came upon what looked to be a fig, lying on the floor in one of the near-empty concourses. On closer inspection I saw that it was a turd—a dog's, most likely. *What has this world come to?* I thought. It was like seeing my office in ruins. The airport was *my* place. I knew its rhythms and its rules, could tell the professional travelers from the novices the moment they stepped from their cars, the latter with their spongy neck pillows holding up the TSA screenings. "I knew I couldn't go through with water, but Sprite too?"

I would be in precheck, not inconvenienced by the novices but incensed nevertheless. I guess you don't realize how good it feels to look down on someone until you've both, indiscriminately, been kicked to the curb.

I couldn't wait to be back on my high horse, and got the

opportunity, finally, in the fall of 2021. My lecture agent had lined up a seventy-two-city tour that was set to begin the second week of September. My old life back, sort of. There would be restrictions: in the states that allowed such things, the audience would have to show proof of vaccination, and everyone would be masked. I tried not to get my hopes up too high, but at the same time I needed to be prepared in case things went my way. If the elephant was indeed going back out with the circus, he needed to be a little bit less of an elephant. I'd gained a good twenty pounds over the past year and a half and would have to lose them if I was going to fit into my tour clothes. The diet I came up with involved walking fifteen miles a day, eating half the amount that I normally did, and filling up on as much sugar-free Jell-O as I wanted.

People asked, "What flavor?"

But there are no flavors, just colors: red, green, yellow, orange, and a new beige one that tasted beige. It was crazy how quickly I lost the weight. Every other week I was taking my belt to the cobbler and having another hole punched. At first he was all, "Congratulations!" Then it was, "*You* again?"

I was just grateful that he recognized me, as I felt that I looked so much older now.

"I think it's your clothes that are the giveaway," Hugh said. And it's true. Think White House–era Harry Truman dressed like White House–era Dolley Madison.

Two days before my tour was to begin, the first city canceled due to fears about the Delta variant. I worried the others would fall like dominoes, but the second, Nashville, held. How thrilling it was to be in front of an audience again, to expend energy and actually feel it reverberating back. To be in a nice hotel! I'd find over the coming three months that many of them had cut back on services—a daily room cleaning now had to be specifically asked for, ostensibly for COVID reasons but really because there were so few housekeepers. In city after city, all I saw were HELP WANTED signs. If McDonald's was offering fourteen dollars an hour, the Taco Bell next door was willing to pay sixteen. Every Starbucks was hiring, every drugstore and supermarket. *Have the people who used to work there died?* I wondered. *Where* was *everyone?*

When a teenager came to my book-signing table, my first question was no longer "When did you last see your parents naked?" but "Do you have a job?"

Nine times out of ten, before the kid could speak, his or her mother would take over. "Tyler is too busy with his schoolwork," or "Kayla just needs to be seventeen now." On several occasions the person would be genderqueer, and the mother would say, "Cedar is taking some time to figure themself out."

There was a Willow as well, and a Hickory. I guessed that was a thing now, naming yourself after a tree.

One woman I met, a mother of three, told me that none of her teenagers held jobs and weren't likely to anytime soon. "Why should they bust their butts for seventeen dollars an hour?"

"Um, because it's seventeen more than they get by sitting at home doing nothing?"

"I grew up having to work and don't want to put my kids in that headspace," the woman said.

Dear God, I thought. *America, as I knew it, is finished.* Aren't you *supposed* to have a shitty job when you're a teenager? It's how you develop a sense of compassion. The three oldest kids in my family worked in cafeterias, while Amy was a supermarket cashier. Tiffany worked in kitchens; Paul too. We made $1.60 an hour and, dammit, we were happy to get it. That's the way this country ran. If, at age sixteen, you wanted a bong, you went out there and worked for it. Now I guess your parents just buy it for you and probably give you the pot as well.

Toward the end of my tour the *New York Times* ran an article about the many schools that were instituting virtual Fridays. Parents were up in arms, as now they'd have to find sitters or stay at home themselves that day. "Well, I think it's much needed," said every teacher I spoke to. "Our jobs are really stressful." Everyone was saying that now. Being a claims adjuster, heading an IT unit, publicizing eye shadow: "It's hard work that takes a real toll on me!"

Because it was so difficult to find and retain staff, people who, two years earlier, might have been fired for one reason or another were still at their posts—the desk clerk at my Richmond, Virginia, hotel, for instance. I arrived shortly after midnight and found the place deserted. Not a soul in the lobby. "Hello!" I called. "Is anybody here?"

When no one answered, I took a step behind the check-in desk and tried again. "Hello?"

I walked to the bell stand and back. I peered into the restaurant, which was closed off with a louvered metal gate. A few minutes passed, and just as I was wondering if I should call a cab and try some other hotel, a woman appeared—midforties, slightly disheveled, and angry. Her mouth was small and looked like a recently healed exit wound. "What are you *doing*?" she demanded. "You're not supposed to step behind my counter, especially now, in COVID times. We can't have people back here!"

"I'm sorry," I said. "There was no one around, and I wasn't sure—"

"We *know* you're *here*," the woman snapped. "We got *cameras*. We can *see* you."

Well, I've never worked in a hotel, I thought. *How am I supposed to know your setup?* "If you saw me, why didn't you come out?" I asked.

"I was *busy*," she said. "Is that OK with you, me doing stuff?"

She'd clearly been lying down. The only question was, had she been alone or with someone else? This wasn't some flophouse that rented rooms by the hour. My one night was costing close to $200, but even if it were one-tenth that price, you can't talk to your guests like that, at least not when they're being reasonably polite.

I decided that on my way out the following morning I was going to tell on this woman, but when the time came and her associate asked, "How was your stay?" I said, simply, "Fine," thinking, as I always do when someone is rude to me, *At least I can write about it.*

Then too I just felt lucky, not only to be back at work but to seemingly have the one job in America that wasn't too much to handle. *There is literally nothing to this,* I'd think every night as I walked from the wings of the stage to the podium, trying not to trip on my floor-length shirt. It had a heavy, braided hem, and I was devastated to realize one afternoon that I'd left it in the closet of the hotel I had checked out of that morning. Of course, I called in the hopes of getting it back, though in retrospect I should have said, "Yes, I'm afraid my wife forgot to pack her nightgown." As it was, the desk clerk kept insisting that what had been turned in was most certainly meant for a woman.

"Look at the tag," I told him. "It says *Homme Plus. Homme* means *man* in French."

"Yes," the person said, "but this is...decorative."

On top of the countless HELP WANTED signs and the many Christian T-shirts I saw people wearing—among them ON MY BLESSED BEHAVIOR and LONG STORY SHORT: GOD SAVED MY LIFE—I noticed how very different it was to go from one state to the next, or even from city to city within a particular state. In Los Angeles, masks were mandatory in all the common areas of my hotel, and I had to show proof of vaccination in order to enter the restaurant. Should I leave for any reason, I'd have to show it again upon my reentry, because this was Los Angeles, where, unless you're either famous or horribly disfigured, no one remembers your face—especially just the top half of it—for more than five seconds, or three if you're over fifty. From there, I went to Palm Springs, where, aside from the staff in their black N95s, my hotel was wide-open. It's worth noting that both of those places were high-end—a Four Seasons and a Ritz-Carlton. From California I flew to Montana. Out of habit I wore a mask into the lobby of my hotel and received the sort of looks I might get had I sported a HILLARY CLINTON T-shirt at a Klan rally. The following afternoon I went to lunch and was shocked that none of the staff had their faces covered: not the hostess or the waiter, and neither of the cooks I could see when the door to the kitchen opened. For much of America—the red parts, primarily—the pandemic was over, at least on the ground, and a mask actually made me feel *un*safe.

Meanwhile, in the air, face coverings were mandatory by federal law. Pilots made regular announcements, but most of the heavy lifting was left to the flight attendants. Sometimes it was a losing battle. On an early-morning plane I took from Odessa, Texas, to Houston, several of my fellow passengers said, politely but firmly, "Nope. I'm done with your regulations." Our flight attendant was all of twenty-three years old, and what could she do, really? When she attempted to scold the guy beside me, he made a comment about her appearance.

"Sir, could I please ask you to cover your nose and mouth?"

"You have a smokin' body."

"I beg your pardon?"

"Nice face too. I'd like to see more of it."

He had put away two double vodkas, and it wasn't even nine a.m. "I'm going to slip that little girl a hundred dollars on my way off the plane," he told me, his voice like tires on gravel, as we touched down. "See if I don't, because that amount of money is nothing to me."

The man was right up in my face, his spittle flecking my glasses, and I thought, *Seriously? I'm going to get my COVID from* you? *Why couldn't it come from someone I like?*

But I didn't get sick. This is remarkable, because I was incredibly reckless. Most nights I removed my mask for the book signings and pushed aside the plexiglass shield that should have stood between me and the person I was talking to. Otherwise it was too hard to be heard or to hear. I rode in crowded elevators and in cars with drivers whose mouths, like my own, more often than not weren't entirely covered. There were venues that strictly enforced the mask policy, which was fine unless they were enforcing it with *me*. I liked a situation in which I took no precautions and the rest of the world was made to double up. I liked to be in a red state, maskless and complaining about how backward everyone around me was.

Tours have always been good for getting me out of my bubble, and this one all the more so. Driving across the Midwest, I saw one TRUMP 2024 sign after another—this while the election was an entire three years away. "You know you're in a place that's inhospitable to liberals when you see fireworks stores," Adam said in rural Indiana as we passed one powder keg after another.

"Fireworks are guns for children," I observed.

"They're the gateway drug," Adam agreed.

Then there were the actual guns—one I saw, for instance, in Dayton, Ohio, as I waited in line to get a cup of coffee. Ahead of me stood a group of three, none of whom had apparently ever been to a Starbucks before. All were bearded and maskless. Theirs were the faces you'd see on a WANTED DEAD OR ALIVE poster in the Old West, but colorized. "What's the closest you got to a milkshake?" the tallest of them asked the odd little being behind the counter. "Is the ice in a Mocha Cookie Crumble Frappuccino shaved or in chunks?"

A month earlier, at a coffee shop in Springfield, Missouri, I saw a sign for an Almond Joy Latte. For all our talk about health and, worse still, "wellness," the burning question in most of America is "How can we make this *more* fattening?" This has long been the case. I was only noticing it because of my recent diet and my losing struggle to keep the weight off. In Des Moines I heard about a restaurant that served hamburgers on buns made from compressed macaroni and cheese. When, in Boston, I saw "Vegan Soup" on a menu, my immediate assumption was not that it contained no butter or cream but that it was made of an actual vegan, the heaviest one they could find and boil.

The group of three in front of me in the Dayton Starbucks all ordered drinks that involved the blender and great mountains of whipped cream. Then the tallest of them wondered if Donna wanted anything. She was out in the car, perhaps bound and gagged in its trunk. As he reached into his rear pocket for his phone, his shirt rose, and I saw that he had a pistol tucked into his jeans. A school shooting had taken place twenty minutes earlier in Oxford Township, Michigan, so the sight spooked me more than it might have a day earlier. *Are he and his friends going to rob this place?* I wondered. Or maybe they'd held up a gas station earlier in the afternoon and were off duty now. I mean, robbers don't rob *every* business they walk into, right?

The America I saw in the fall of 2021 was weary and battle-scarred. Its sidewalks were cracked. Its mailboxes bashed in. All along the West Coast I saw tent cities. They were in parks, in vacant lots and dilapidated squares. In one stop after another I'd head to a store or restaurant I remembered and find it boarded up, or maybe burned out, the plywood that blocked the doors covered with graffiti: EAT THE RICH. FUCK THE POLICE. BLACK LIVES MATTER.

During my year and a half at home, I had forgotten about the ups and downs of life on tour. One night you're at Symphony Hall, and the next in a worn-out, once grand movie theater that is now overrun by mice. "Can you believe they wanted to tear this place down?" the house manager invariably asks, fondly looking up at a gold plaster cherub with one arm missing.

"Um, yes, as a matter of fact."

It's the same with hotels. From the new Four Seasons in Philadelphia, I went to a Four Points by Sheraton on the side of an eight-lane road in York, Pennsylvania. It was a Friday, and all the guests had tattoos on their necks except me and a very angry mother of the bride, who had hers—two smudged butterflies—hovering above her right ankle. My room was at the rear of the building, and every time I looked out my window, I saw people gathered in the parking lot. *Is there a fire drill I missed?* I'd wonder.

The following morning, I went out back to see what the fuss was about and found a pile of human shit beside a face mask someone had wiped their ass on.

At noon it was off to the Ritz-Carlton in Washington, DC. The next day, at breakfast in the ground-floor restaurant, I watched as a woman at the table beside me asked for an extra plate. This she loaded with bacon and eggs, and set upon the carpet so that her little terrier could eat from it.

Honestly? I thought. *On the carpet?* After the dog had finished his breakfast, he strayed. People's paths were blocked by his extendable leash, but no one except me—who had remained seated and thus was not actually inconvenienced—seemed to mind. "Oh my God!" my fellow guests cried, as if it were a baby panda they had stumbled upon. "How adorable are you?" One woman announced that she had two fur babies waiting for her at home.

"It must kill you to be separated from them," the whore who'd set the plate on the carpet said.

"Oh, it does," admitted the jism-soaked hag who had started the conversation. "But they'll see Mommy soon enough."

Was feeding your dog from a plate in the dining room better than wiping your ass on a face mask? Difficult to say, really. Both were pretty hard to take. That said, if you're after a decent night's sleep, your safest bet is the Ritz, where most of the guests have at least stayed in a hotel before and know better than to yell, "Bro, you are *so* fucking high right now!" outside your door at three a.m.

Whenever the extremes got to me, I'd comfort myself with the many interesting people I met as I made my way across the country—a woman, for instance, whose father had executed her pet hamster with a .22 rifle.

"But why?" I asked.

"Butterscotch had a virus that caused all her hair to fall out," she told me.

Then there was the psychologist whose father's last words to her, croaked out on his deathbed, were "You are a communist cunt."

The most haunting person was one I never met face-to-face. In the middle of my tour I was to fly from Springfield, Missouri, to Chicago, where I would have a night off. I arrived at the airport early, checked my bag, and was walking out-doors, getting some steps in, when I received the message that my flight—that all flights to Chicago—had been canceled. And so I asked if a car could possibly be arranged. One was, and while I waited for it to arrive, I got some more steps in. Because I had to keep an eye on my luggage, I couldn't go far, so I walked circles around the baggage carousels, none of which were in use. Passing one of them, I saw, huddled in its gutter, two pairs of soiled panties; a nearly empty Tic Tac dispenser; a brush with strands of long, strawberry-blond hair caught in it; three AA batteries; and a little sheaf of toothpicks. It was such an interesting portrait of someone—a young woman, I assumed—and I thought of her for months to come, wondering, as I moved from place to place in this divided, beat-up country of ours, where she was and what she imagined had become of her panties.